CELEBRATING HOLIDAYS
SCRAPBOOK-STYLE

250 sensational page ideas you can create

know what it is to be a child?
it is to be
so little
that the elves
can reach to
whisper
in your ear.

— Francis Thompson

MEMORY
MAKERS
BOOKS

Executive Editor Kerry Arquette   *Founder* Michele Gerbrandt

Senior Editor Lydia Rueger

Art Director Andrea Zocchi

Graphic Designers Nick Nyffeler, Jennifer Pollman

Art Aquisitions Editor Janetta Abucejo Wieneke

Craft Editor Jodi Amidei

Photographer Ken Trujillo

Contributing Photographer Jennifer Reeves

Contributing Writer Brandi Ginn, Kari Hansen-Daffin

Contributing Artist Torrey Miller

Editorial Support Karen Cain, Emily Curry Hitchingham, MaryJo Regier, Dena Twinem, Heather Wells

Contributing Memory Makers Masters Valerie Barton, Joanna Bolick, Susan Cyrus, Brandi Ginn, Torry Miller, Kelli Noto, Trudy Sigurdson, Denise Tucker, Andrea Lyn Vetten-Marley, Sharon Whitehead

Published by Memory Makers Books, an imprint of F+W Publications, Inc.

12365 Huron Street, Suite 500, Denver, CO 80234

Phone (800) 254-9124

First edition. Printed in the United States.

08 07 06 05 04 5 4 3 2 1

Library of Congress Cataloging-in-Publication Data

Celebrating holidays scrapbook-style : 250 sensational page ideas you can create.
      p.cm.
   Includes bibliographical references and index.
   ISBN 1-892127-27-X
   1. Photographs--Conversation and restoration. 2. Photograph albums. 3. Scrapbooks. 4.
Scrapbook journaling. 5. Holiday decorations. I. Memory Makers Books.

   TR465.C372826 2004
   745. 593--dc22

                                                         2004050473

Distributed to trade and art markets by

F+W Publications, Inc.

4700 East Galbraith Road, Cincinnati, OH 45236

Phone 1-800-289-0963

ISBN 1-892127-27-X

Memory Makers Books is the home of *Memory Makers*, the scrapbook magazine dedicated to educating and inspiring scrapbookers. To subscribe, or for more information, call (800) 366-6465.

Visit us on the Internet at www.memorymakersmagazine.com.

This book belongs to

Dedicated to scrapbookers who strive to preserve holiday traditions in their homes. May your holiday pages project the same feelings of warmth and magic that you help create each season.

Table of CONTENTS

Together at Christmas

2003 Christmas at Pam and Tony's ~ 2003
With families spread out between Colorado, Oregon, and California, getting everyone together at Christmas takes a lot of effort. It was crazy having 13 people in one house for 5 days, but it just felt right. We sang carols, made Russian pancakes on Christmas Eve, read the Christmas story together from the Bible and went bargain hunting on December 26... wouldn't have wanted it any other way!

25
Christmas Day

Merry Christmas ✶ Merry Christmas ✶

Introduction

Year after year, as one holiday tumbles onto the heels of the next, it seems I can never have enough inspiration for holiday layouts. I want each successive page I create to look different from those I created the year before, reflecting my children's growth and our evolving traditions. Because each years' celebrations are unique, I try not to fall back on previously-used page layouts and titles. My best inspirations for fresh page ideas come from our readers who offer interesting photo perspectives, creatively-presented journaling and cutting-edge designs. I find myself borrowing a border idea from one reader and a title treatment from another to create holiday pages that are unique to the memories and emotions of that year.

I'm sure the ideas in *Celebrating Holidays Scrapbook-Style* will inspire you to create novel holiday pages throughout the year too. You'll find tons of new spins on well-known holidays such as Christmas, Halloween and the 4th of July, but you'll also discover ideas for lesser-known holidays such as Martin Luther King Jr. Day and Veterans Day.

In addition to 250 terrific scrapbook page ideas created by some of the nation's top scrapbook artists, we've included fun facts and legends throughout the book that can be used to kick-start layout concepts. We figure the more you know about the holidays you celebrate, the more creativity will flow when it's time to make pages about them. And because scrapbookers are always looking to better understand design concepts no matter the time of year, we've included tips that will help you make good layouts great.

Holidays bring out the child in all of us. I tend to get as excited as my children do at the thought of Christmas morning or fireworks exploding in a coal-black sky. And watching my children experience these special events makes the holidays all the more precious. Now, thanks to the ideas in *Celebrating Holidays Scrapbook-Style*, I'm just as excited for the calmer days following my favorite celebrations, knowing that I can revisit those events when I scrapbook them.

Michele

Michele Gerbrandt
Founder
Memory Makers magazine

Making a Good Layout Great

Successful holiday events rarely run smoothly without careful thought and preparation. The same is true with holiday layouts that stand out as especially well-done. If you find yourself making "good enough" layouts but would like to make them great, here are several basic design principles you can follow. These principles, when paired with your own creative ideas and style, will allow you to execute pages that pop every time.

Emphasis: *Creating a point of focus that attracts attention.*

Enlarging the single best photo in a related group gives it emphasis over other page elements and creates a place to draw one's eye. Christine MacIlvaine of Oakland, New Jersey, demonstrates emphasis well on this computer-generated layout. She enlarged her favorite photo as well as making it black and white to set it apart from the smaller photographs.

Unity: *Creating agreement among page elements.*

Carly Christopher of Bellingham, Washington, unified this page by using small amounts of the same patterned papers in multiple places. Using a variety of patterns from the same Chatterbox line made coordinating easy.

Balance: *Creating equal distribution of visual weight.*

Jennifer Bourgeault of Macomb Township, Michigan, balanced a prominent title at the top of this Valentine's Day page with a strong photo border along the bottom. In addition, Jennifer distributed visual weight evenly by positioning journaling directly across from an enlarged photo in the center of her page.

Proportion and scale: *Building the relationship of objects according to their size and placement.*

To accent her multiple-choice-style journaling, Jennifer chose small heart-shaped buttons that are proportionate to the size of her font. The type size used at the bottom of the page was chosen to neatly fill the square.

Rhythm: *Repeating recurring motifs to create movement.*

Teddi von Pingel of Mesa, Arizona, creates rhythm on this Easter page by repeating small circles throughout. The circles serve as a background design as well as places for photos and title letters.

Craftsmanship: *Keeping it neat.*

A great layout should be neat and tidy in all aspects. Don't let things like stray pencil lines, visible adhesive, ragged craft knife work or smudges detract from a well-designed layout. Moreover, your page construction should be sturdy enough to stand the test of time.

Making a Good Layout Great

Journaling and title

Journaling can sometimes be a struggle, but no layout is complete without it. Your journaling should always answer the questions who, what, when, where, why and how in some way. To take your journaling to the next level, include details that one can visualize and personal thoughts. You may have heard an English teacher say, "show, don't tell" in class long ago—apply this concept to your scrapook journaling. Instead of saying "We were surprised to get snow on Halloween," for example, describe how snow in October looks, as Peggy Roarty of Council Bluffs, Iowa, did on the page above. Her sentence "The trees, still laden with fall leaves, all stood frail and haggard from the heaviness of the ice" provides a vivid description of her yard on that day.

In addition to journaling, your page title should capture the essence of the photos, give an overview of the layout and draw interest. While simple, Peggy's title, "White Halloween," is intriguing because white is not normally used to describe a holiday associated with orange pumpkins and bright fall leaves. Had she chosen the title "Halloween 1997," it would have been sufficient, but less interesting to the reader.

Photos

The core of a great layout is good-quality photos. The most precious handmade embellishments or cutting-edge design can't make up for a lack in this area. Photos should be clear, well-composed, engaging and should help tell the story of the page, like these photos by Amy Stultz of Mooresville, Indiana. For example, when photographing holiday cookie baking, don't just take a few shots of mixing the dough. Photograph all steps in the process, from rolling the dough to cutting out the cookie shapes to decorating them. Zoom in to capture the concentration on a child's face as she decorates. Capture the moment when a child sneaks a taste of the icing. Don't forget to take a picture of the finished project to wrap up the "story" that your photos tell.

Applying Layout Concepts

The pages below are broken down to illustrate how certain design concepts can improve your layouts.
Apply these examples to make good pages great every time.

Jodi Amidei, Memory Makers Books
Photos: Shannon Taylor, Bristol, Tennessee

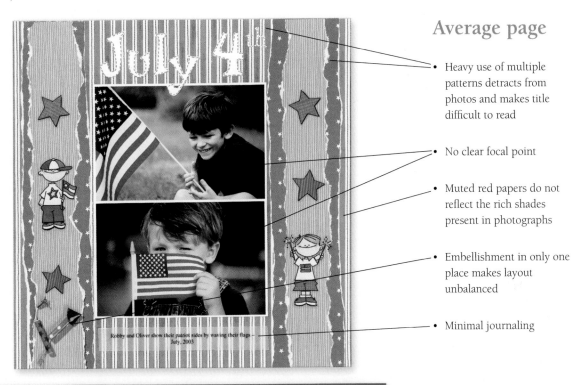

Average page

- Heavy use of multiple patterns detracts from photos and makes title difficult to read

- No clear focal point

- Muted red papers do not reflect the rich shades present in photographs

- Embellishment in only one place makes layout unbalanced

- Minimal journaling

Successful page

- Title designed with multiple elements creates interest

- Enlarged photo creates emphasis

- Personal, thought-provoking journaling

- Colors and patterns complement photos

- Dainty star embellishments repeated across layout to unify the page

adore

Believe IN THE

The Christmas season once again found tiny Tucker tots with their eyes all aglow as they awaited a visit with Santa Clause. (December 2001)

MAGIC

of *Christmas*

Happy New Year!

kiss

love

Connor, Devon and Jemma getting an early start on the 2004 New Year celebration!

Winter HOLIDAYS

When sunlit hours are limited, the air bites with cold and your coziest socks never seem to be enough, moments found in winter holidays can provide the warmth you need. There's kisses on New Year's, chocolate that melts in your mouth on Valentine's Day and steaming dinners and candlelight during the Christmas season. Hand-holding and hugging abound amidst the chill no matter what holiday is being celebrated. In more ways than Santa Claus is different from a leprechaun, this chapter offers tons of ideas for documenting your winter holiday celebrations.

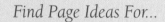

Find Page Ideas For...

*Ever since we started
spending time together,
I've had a really good feeling
about you and me.*

*Maybe it's because we seem
to get along in so many ways,
or that I want to share
so much with you.*

*Or maybe it's because
whenever I'm around you,
time just seems to fly by.*

*Whatever it is,
it sure feels good.*

-- Linda Lee Elrod

January

Mary used a monochromatic color scheme with black-and-white photos to create an elegant New Year's design. Cut 2" strips of embossed paper and layer along inside edges of patterned paper background. Create large frames by layering patterned paper on light blue cardstock. Print title and journaling on patterned vellum and attach to page with blue eyelets. Attach photos with photo corners to dark blue cardstock, mat again with light blue and tear along one edge. Color torn edges with silver marker and tie each mat with sheer ribbon. Accent small photo with metal frame and charm.

Mary Walby, Royal Oak, Michigan
Photos: Kathryn Smith, Farmington Hills, Michigan

Supplies: Dark blue textured cardstock (Bazzill); flower patterned paper and vellum (EK Success); embossed paper (Paper Diva); snowflake stamp (Paper Inspirations); metal frame and snowflake charm (Making Memories); light blue cardstock; stamping ink; photo corners; ribbon

January

12/31/02

Not all the members of Stacy's family make it to midnight on New Year's Eve, which she documents here. Print title and journaling on cream cardstock and stamp with clock face images. Tear and layer orange cardstock and patterned paper; roll back the edges. Tear slots in patterned paper and cardstock; slip photo into slots. Accent page with watch crystals filled with clock and watch parts.

Stacy Hackett, Murrieta, California

Supplies: Patterned paper (Bo-Bunny Press); stamp (Club Scrap); watch crystals and gears (Jest Charming); brad; cream and orange cardstocks; stamping ink

National Tin Foil Day

The Heslops exchange presents on New Year's Day, coined "National Tin Foil Day," because Catherine wraps presents in foil when the Christmas wrap is used up. Crop and mat three photos on dark gray cardstock and layer on metallic paper background. Print title on gray vellum, write journaling and attach to page with silver brads.

Catherine Heslop, Brights Grove, Ontario, Canada

Supplies: Metallic paper, gray cardstock and vellum (Suburban Paper); black pen; brads

National Tin Foil Day

I am so good at hiding Christmas presents that sometimes I cannot find them. That is how the tradition began of giving the children presents on New Years Day. They began calling it National Tin Foil Day when I started wrapping the presents in tin foil because there was no wrapping paper left over from Christmas. Now we all look forward to Tin Foil Day, the weird thing is that every year I do hide someone's gift and find it after Christmas. They try to figure out whose present was the forgotten one.

Supplies: Flower patterned paper (EK Success); fibers (On The Surface); frame (Patchwork Paper); label holder and brad (Making Memories); brown and green papers

New Year's Eve

Kate and her husband celebrated the New Year at a French restaurant complete with a seven-course meal. Tear brown and green papers and mat on patterned paper, leaving open space at the bottom. Frame picture with premade frame and accent with brads. Print journaling and accent journaling block with premade corner accent and brad. Embellish page using metal label holder adorned with fibers.

Kate Nelson, Fountain, Colorado

Seafood Feast

A family tradition of seafood for New Year's Eve has been a favorite of Brandi's since she was young. Tear and layer patterned papers on purple cardstock to create the background; repeat technique for photo mat. Mat other photo on oversized yellow cardstock, stitch on buttons and chalk all edges. Chalk edges of journaling block and layer with journaling printed on a transparency; accent with fibers and word tiles. Die cut title letters from purple and yellow. Place one letter on a square tag and adhere with dimensional adhesive.

Brandi Ginn, Lafayette, Colorado

Supplies: Yellow and purple textured cardstocks (Bazzill); purple patterned paper (Scrap Ease); yellow patterned paper (All My Memories); die-cut letters (QuicKutz); square tag (Making Memories); tile words and buttons (Junkitz); fibers (Fiber Scraps); transparency (Grafix); dimensional adhesive; chalk

Supplies: Pink, taupe and patterned papers (SEI); word pebbles (Making Memories); number pebbles (Li'l Davis Designs); metal letters (All My Memories); vellum; brads; image-editing software

Looking Back...Looking Forward

Jodi reflects on her blessings over the past year and focuses on her goals for the year to come. Cut geometric shapes of patterned paper and piece together to form a mosaic on the bottom half of each page. Layer thin strips of pink and taupe paper on pink cardstock background at top, center and bottom of spread. Print journaling on vellum and adhere with silver brads; accent with page pebbles. Using image-editing software, reduce the color saturation of one picture revealing lighter shades. Reverse the image and lighten again. Print photos in four different sizes. For title, place small squares of patterned paper behind clear number pebbles and adhere metal letters.

Jodi Amidei, Memory Makers Books

Facts & Legends:

Before New York's famous New Year's Eve ball-lowering celebration, the first ceremony to take place on the roof of One Times Square was held in 1904 to commemorate the New York Times' new headquarters. The first New Year's celebration atop the same building was held on December 31, 1907. Now constructed of Waterford crystal, colored lights, halogen bulbs and strobe lights, the first New Year's ball was made of wood, iron and 100 25-watt bulbs.

Try This:

Use small mirrored embellishments on a New Year's page to represent Times Square's famous crystal ball. Place mirrors in a circle to make the New Year's ball itself or arrange the pieces for a shining, festive page border.

I Have a Dream

Gemiel's family celebrates Martin Luther King Jr. Day by reading books and discussing his achievements. To pay tribute to the holiday in her scrapbook, Gemiel made a spread about a visit to Dr. King's hometown. Crop photos to create a photo border along the bottom of both sides. Double mat other photos and adhere to patterned background. Using metal stamps, add word to metal sheet, cut into tag shape and punch holes in tag. Attach tag and yarn to one photo mat and words cut from memorabilia to another mat. Print journaling on vellum and adhere to page. Add letter stickers for title. Embellish slide mount with metal charm.

Gemiel Matthews, Yorktown, Virginia

Supplies: Patterned paper, cardstock and letter stickers (Club Scrap); slide mount (www.scrapsahoy.com); charm (All The Extras); metal tag (AMACO); metal stamps; yarn; memorabilia

Defining Our Boxing Day

Colleen's family celebrates Boxing Day by enjoying one another's company. Tear patterned paper along one edge and layer on black cardstock. Place enlarged photo on upper left side and layer with metal plaques, dimensional letters and title block. Mat remaining photos on black cardstock and place at angles on page, adhering one with dimensional adhesive. Create title block using stickers, dimensional letters and brads. Print journaling on cream cardstock, cut out and ink edges. Accent with stickers, brads, metal letters and dimensional embellishments.

Colleen Macdonald, Calgary, Alberta, Canada

Supplies: Patterned paper, metal letters, metal plaques and bubble phrases (Li'l Davis Designs); letter stickers (Me & My Big Ideas); stickers (Sticker Studio); black cardstock; brads; dimensional adhesive

Boxing Day

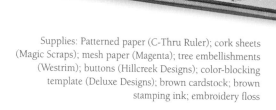

Celebrating Boxing Day

Trudy's family celebrates Boxing Day each year by going to her cousin's house for dinner and exchanging gifts. Mat photos on brown paper and ink the edges with stamping ink. Use a color-blocking template to arrange photos and other page elements on patterned paper. Tear cork and ink the edges with stamping ink; layer with mesh and add journaling blocks, buttons and tree accents. Print title on light brown paper, ink edges and stitch around edges. Embellish title block by attaching square letters with mini buttons.

Trudy Sigurdson, Victoria, British Columbia, Canada

Supplies: Patterned paper (C-Thru Ruler); cork sheets (Magic Scraps); mesh paper (Magenta); tree embellishments (Westrim); buttons (Hillcreek Designs); color-blocking template (Deluxe Designs); brown cardstock; brown stamping ink; embroidery floss

Facts & Legends:

Celebrated in Great Britain, Canada, Australia and New Zealand, Boxing Day reportedly began because servants had to work on Christmas Day. On December 26, the servants' employers would give them boxes of gifts before they left to spend the day with their families. Today, Boxing Day is celebrated by spending time with family, shopping and donating to charitable organizations.

Try This:

Cut brown paper into squares and rectangles and tie each with string to create page accents that resemble boxes. Fold and score the top edge of each "box" and attach them over your photos to make flip-up elements.

Reasons I'm Attracted to You

When Marpy's husband brought home a plastic cover from a car's headlight, she used it on a page about their relationship. Layer patterned paper and shattered plastic piece on green background. Alter photo with image-editing software, print out and mat on red. Cover library pocket with patterned paper and stickers; write reasons on premade number strips and place in pocket. Attach paint chip across bottom. Print title on transparency and heat emboss. Stamp and heat emboss angels, silhouette and layer over paint chip.

Marpy Hayse, Katy, Texas

Supplies: Patterned paper (Karen Foster Design); cherub and magnet stamps (Rubber Baby Buggy Bumpers); number strips (Sweetwater); word and letter stickers (Sweetwater, Pebbles); image-editing software (Adobe Photoshop); green cardstock; paint chip; transparency; stamp library pocket; stamping ink; plastic piece; embossing powder

Bouquet of Love

Gifts are not often exchanged between Angie and her husband, so when he surprised her with flowers on Valentine's Day, she wanted to capture the moment. Place enlarged photo in upper right-hand corner of black cardstock. Print title and journaling on vellum and place vellum over picture. Crop photos and accent with strips of patterned paper. Crop additional photos small enough to fit inside square tags and embellish with heart-shaped brads.

Angie Cramer, Redcliff, Alberta, Canada

Supplies: Word patterned paper (7 Gypsies); metal-rimmed tags (Making Memories); black cardstock; heart brads; vellum

How Do I Love Thee?

Libby created a layout to match one of her daughter's valentine presents. Ink the edges of brown cardstock and all patterned papers with black ink. Layer leopard paper and red patterned paper on brown cardstock. Place a 1" strip on black cardstock at each end. Rub brown ink on brown cardstock. Mat photos on black cardstock. Write journaling on background. Accent with preprinted accents and fibers.

Libby Weifenbach, Bentonville, Arkansas

Supplies: Red patterned paper and preprinted accents (Bo-Bunny Press); leopard paper (Making Memories); fibers (Friendly Fibers); brown and black cardstocks; stamping inks; black pen

Facts & Legends:

The first "valentine" is said to have been sent from an imprisoned bishop named Valentine to his jailer's daughter on the night before he was executed for refusing to denounce Christianity. The jailer's daughter delivered food and messages for Valentine. The note was signed "From your Valentine."

Another legend surrounding the holiday's origin talks of a third-century Roman emperor who outlawed marriage because he believed single men without family attachments made better soldiers. A priest named Valentine defied the order and performed marriage ceremonies in secret. When discovered, the emperor ordered that Valentine be put to death.

Try This:

Save valentine cards you receive and use them as ready-made page accents. Mat a single card with coordinating paper to match your page, or punch small shapes from multiple cards as a border design.

Valentine Be Mine

Valerie created a layout with vintage charm by combining patterned papers and textures in coordinating styles. Place a 2" strip of harlequin patterned paper over red patterned background. Mat photo on patterned paper and place on top of paper strip. Create title by first applying letter stickers to background. Tear vellum and patterned paper along one side and machine stitch to background. Place metal word on top of vellum; accent with circle tag, patterned paper, heart charm and embroidery floss. Finish title by placing other metal words on background. Print journaling on tag, crumple and flatten, then decorate with ribbon and small tag. Fold vellum and patterned paper to form an envelope; place journaling tag inside. Decorate envelope with ribbon, ribbon charm, eyelets and letter bead. Stamp a vintage label for name and age. Accent punched heart shape with wire and adhere to page with foam tape. Add metal phrase.

Valerie Salmon, Carmel, Indiana
Photo: JC Penney Portraits, Indianapolis, Indiana

Supplies: Patterned papers (Sarah Lugg); metal words, phrase and ribbon charm (Making Memories); tag (Avery); rubber stamp (Anna Griffin); heart punch (Emagination Crafts); letter stickers (EK Success); ribbon; vellum; black stamping ink; embroidery floss; heart charm; letter bead; black pen

Love Is in the Air

When Linda's grandchildren stopped by on Valentine's Day, she just couldn't resist taking pictures of them in their matching shirts. Layer red plaid paper over purple cardstock. Mat photos on purple cardstock and adhere to page. Tear a strip of purple patterned paper and mount on bottom of page, slightly covering the pictures. Accent torn purple strip with preprinted tag and border. Print journaling on vellum, tear edges and attach with buttons. Mat preprinted title with purple cardstock. Embellish heart accent by applying adhesive to the front of the heart and pressing on clear glass marbles. Mount heart accent at corner of title. Mount remaining preprinted accents to a torn purple square with foam tape.

Linda Beeson, Ventura, California

Supplies: Patterned papers, preprinted accents and buttons (Two Busy Moms); purple cardstock; foam tape

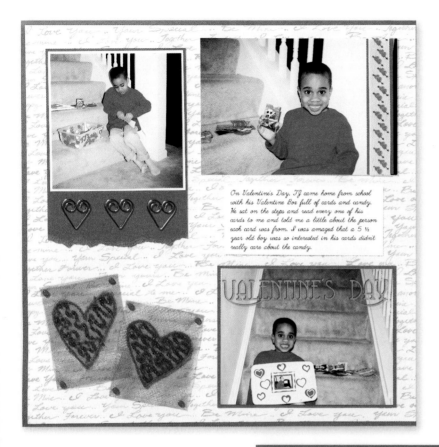

Valentine's Day

Gemiel made a vellum pocket to store her son's valentine cards and to document his fascination with the cards. Create left page by layering script paper over red cardstock. Mat photos with cream and red. Accent photos with heart clips and ribbon and apply a word sticker over one photo. Embellish page with beaded hearts attached to mesh and adhered with red brads. Create right page by matting a single photo on cream, red, and script papers; add red beads and a heart charm. Fold a piece of vellum into a pocket and insert valentines. Print journaling and mat on cream. Accent journaling block with metal heart charms, torn paper and ribbon.

Gemiel Matthews, Yorktown, Virginia

Supplies: Script patterned paper (Carolee's Creations); heart clips (Making Memories); word sticker (EK Success); poem (My Mind's Eye); wine glass charm and beaded hearts (Target); bead trim (Jo-Ann Fabric); ribbon; brads; vellum; red and cream cardstocks

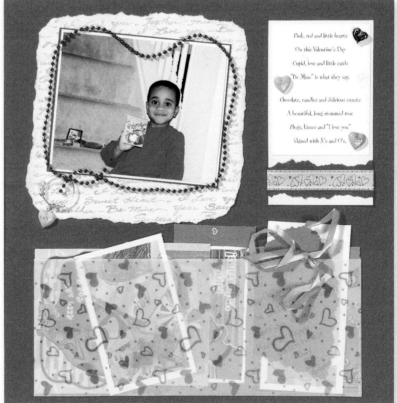

Grandma and Her Lucky Glasses

Sharon recounts a series of "lucky" events that enabled her mother to survive a heart attack right before St. Patrick's Day. Punch shamrock shapes from shades of green. Add buttons, brads and chalk to shamrocks and adhere all to green cardstock. Attach selected shamrocks with foam tape. Cut shamrock-decorated paper into mats for two photos. Double mat other shamrocks and buttons on small squares; apply to page along with thin green strips. Create title by bending fabric-covered wire into letters. Print journaling on white cardstock and accent with green chalks.

Sharon Whitehead, Vernon, British Columbia, Canada

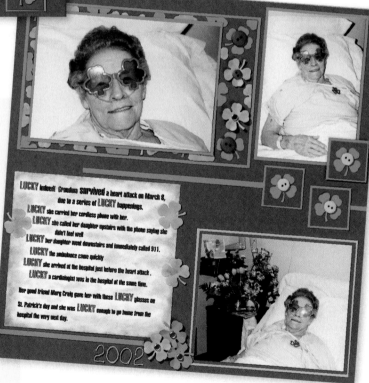

Facts & Legends:

The man commonly known as St. Patrick was born in Roman Britain, kidnapped at age 16 and sold into slavery in Ireland. He worked as a shepherd for six years before escaping to find his homeland. He became a priest and, many years later, returned to Ireland as a missionary. Legend has it that Patrick used the three-leaf shamrock to explain the concept of the Christian Trinity (Father, Son and Holy Spirit) to the Irish people.

Try This:

Form three-leaf clovers from polymer clay and add to a page to represent a concept from Patrick's days as a missionary. While the clay is still moist, poke two holes in the center. When dry, thread embroidery floss through the holes for handmade St. Patrick's Day buttons.

Supplies: Shamrock punch (Marvy); buttons (Making Memories); chalk (Craf-T); fabric wire (Darice); brads; foam tape; green cardstocks

Supplies: Patterned papers
(Hot Off The Press); preprinted
quote (EK Success); paper yarn
(Making Memories); letter beads
(Darice); black cardstock; wire;
mulberry paper; mini clothespin

A Pound of Pluck

Inspired by the preprinted quote, Tiffany collaged squares to match. Mat photos on black cardstock
and adhere to patterned paper. Tie paper yarn around one photo. Layer cardstock with small pieces of
patterned paper, paper yarn and mulberry paper; cut into three squares. Add letter beads, wire and a preprinted shamrock to the squares. Print journaling on white paper, cut into three rectangles and layer over
black gingham paper. Hang preprinted quote from main photo with mini clothespin and paper yarn.

Tiffany Roberts, Bonny Lake, Washington

St. Patrick's Day 2003

Robin created a playful mood on her page by designing
her journaling with different fonts and embellishments.
Cut strip of black cardstock and adhere to left side of
patterned background. Place shorter, wider strip of green
cardstock next to black strip. Mat photo on oversized
piece of black cardstock and layer over green. Print title
on white, cut out and apply to top right-hand corner of
photo mat. Format journaling in different fonts, print
out and cut apart. Add words to black strip, embellishing selected words with tags, charms, brads, fibers and
eyelets. Decorate accent tag by layering with green paper
and inking the edges. Apply shamrock clip art and wrap
with wire strung with beads. Set eyelets and add wire,
charms and buttons.

Robin Hohenstern, Brooklyn Park, Minnesota

Supplies: Patterned paper (Ever After); vellum tags (Making Memories); circle tag
(Avery); charms (found at local dollar store); shamrock clip art (Broderbund); green
and black cardstocks; fibers; buttons; beads; wire; brads

It's Not So Funny Being Green

Leah dressed the family dogs in little green hats for St. Patrick's Day. Trim edges of patterned paper and ink the edges of patterned paper and green cardstock; layer. Mat photos on peach, pink and green cardstocks and adhere to page at angles. Create title by cutting letters from colored cardstocks with a craft knife. Print journaling on cardstock and crop into a circle. Embellish page with smaller circles layered with stickers and stamped words.

Leah Blanco Williams, Kansas City, Missouri

Supplies: Peach and pink textured cardstocks (Bazzill); patterned paper (Frances Meyer); letter stamps (Hero Arts); date stamp (Making Memories); shamrock stickers (Hambly Studios); stamping ink

Luck of the Irish

Participating in the St. Louis St. Patrick's Day parade is a favorite tradition for Brandi's friend's daughters. Layer striped paper on green cardstock. Cut a 4" strip of checkered paper and layer over striped paper. Mount photos on page. Attach thin strips of patterned paper above and below one photo with silver brads. Print journaling on a transparency and paint the back with white acrylic paint. Cut rectangle from corrugated cardstock and chalk edges. Add die-cut letters, circle tags and shamrocks.

Brandi Ginn, Lafayette, Colorado

Supplies: Striped paper (Pebbles); checked paper (Lasting Impressions); letter die cuts (QuicKutz); green paper; brads; transparency; acrylic paint; chalk

St. Baldrick's

In an effort to raise research money for children with cancer, several members of the Amidei family, including Jodi's husband, shave their heads each year on St. Patrick's Day. Tear two sheets of patterned papers diagonally and mount in opposite corners on green cardstock. Using a template, stitch around the edges of spread with embroidery floss. Crop and mat photos, brushing two colors of acrylic paint across two photo mats. Cut shamrocks from patterned paper and place on page. To create shamrock buttons, roll air-drying clay ¼" thick. Use a shape cutter to cut shamrocks from the clay and poke two small holes in each one. Allow clay to dry and paint with three colors of acrylic paint. For variegated appearance, remove some paint with a baby wipe while paint is still wet. Thread embroidery floss through holes in shamrocks and adhere to page. Print journaling on vellum. For title, die cut letters, apply acrylic paint and accent letters with dimensional glue.

Jodi Amidei, Memory Makers Books

Supplies: Patterned papers and clay (Provo Craft); letter die cuts (QuicKutz); acrylic paint (Delta); dimensional glue (Plaid); stitching template (Timeless Touches); stamping ink; green cardstock; vellum; embroidery floss

Hanukkah

Hanukkah Happenings

Melissa added 3-D stickers to provide detail on a simple color-blocked layout. Cut two strips of blue patterned paper and adhere across the top of blue cardstock background. Apply letter stickers to blue patterned strips for title. Crop and arrange photos, then cut small blocks of green, pink and blue patterned papers to fill space around photos. Apply stickers to patterned-paper blocks.

Melissa Ackerman, Princeton, New Jersey

Facts & Legends:

The Hanukkah celebration centers around a nine-branched candle holder known as the menorah. Jews light one candle for each night of Hanukkah (eight nights total); the ninth branch holds the candle that lights all the others. The significance of the menorah and the eight-day observance is based on the story of a small army that defeated a powerful and oppressive Syrian army, regaining the right to practice their religion. After their victory, the small army restored the Temple, but found they had very little oil with which to light the menorah. The oil should have burned up by nightfall, but miraculously, the candles remained lit for eight days until new oil could arrive.

Supplies: Green and peach patterned cardstocks (Crafter's Workshop); blue patterned paper (Colors by Design); large letter and number stickers (Colorbök); small letter stickers (Provo Craft); Hanukkah stickers (EK Success); blue cardstock

Try This:

Photograph the lighting of the menorah on all eight nights, alternating family members or friends each night. Include all eight photos on a layout to emphasize the importance of candle lighting through repetition.

Joshua's Hanukkiyah

Linda created a layout about her son's new menorah, complete with his handwritten journaling. Layer patterned vellum on purple paper. Create candle border by cutting strips of patterned paper and pieces of yellow vellum. Print title on yellow and cut apart. Construct fold-out element by folding purple cardstock in half and adhering patterned paper to the top. Journal on left side of white cardstock and mount inside fold-out. Crop and mat photos and adhere inside flap. Add punched shapes and strip of patterned paper on upper inside flap. Adhere fold-out to center of page.

Linda Abrams, Thornhill, Ontario, Canada

Supplies: Patterned vellum (Hot Off The Press); Hanukkah patterned paper (source unknown); Jewish-theme punches (McGill); purple, yellow, white and blue cardstocks; clear photo corners

Supplies: Patterned paper (KI Memories); button (Hillcreek Designs); red, brown, and gold cardstocks

Not Forgotten

Nicole made this page for a friend. She chose this page title to represent the Hanukkah story as well as the passing of her friend's father. Print title on brown cardstock, cut into a strip and mount over red cardstock with thinner gold paper strips. Accent title with heart matted on red and gold. Layer mats of brown, red and patterned paper to create background for fold-out photo. Fold gold paper in half to create base for fold-out and adhere enlarged photo on top. Mount another photo inside. Print journaling on brown, cut out and mount inside fold-out. Mount fold-out to page and attach a small rectangle of cardstock and a button for fold-out "handle."

Nicole Cholet, Beaconsfield, Quebec, Canada
Photos: Natalie Weiser, Dollard Des Ormeaux, Quebec, Canada

Our Chanukah Party

Kathi used clean symmetrical lines and bits of sparkle to display her family's traditions. Cut strips of dark purple cardstock for left and right sides of page. Apply ink to edges of strips, add gold embossing powder and heat emboss. Punch squares from metallic patterned paper and adhere to strips. Layer with die-cut shapes. Crop photos into same-size squares, mount on dark purple cardstock and place along bottom of spread. Mat enlarged photos and smaller cropped photos on light purple cardstock and mount on patterned paper. Die cut letters and numbers for title. Print journaling on vellum and adhere over one photo.

Kathi Rerek, Scotch Plains, New Jersey

Supplies: Metallic patterned paper (Club Scrap); letter, dreidel and Star of David die cuts (QuicKutz); gold embossing powder; embossing ink; square punch; vellum; purple cardstocks

Dreidel

Valerie's Hanukkah page highlights the significance of the dreidel game—a part of the Hanukkah celebration. Cut a strip of handmade paper and layer on blue cardstock. Weave ribbon through metal buttons and create a border along the bottom. Mat photos on dark blue cardstock and place on page. Randomly place dreidel stickers throughout design and accent with definition strips. Complete title by brushing acrylic paint in the grooves of metal letters and wiping away the excess. Print journaling on a transparency and brush acrylic paint on the back. Crop one photo to enclose in small metal frame, also painted with acrylic paint. Embellish with circle clips and small tag stamped with date.

Valerie Barton, Flowood, Mississippi

Supplies: Handmade paper (Magenta); metal letters, spiral clips, definitions, date stamp and metal frame (Making Memories); buttons (Blumenthal Lansing); dreidel stickers (EK Success); ribbon; acrylic paint; blue cardstock; stamping ink

Kwanzaa

Kwanzaa 2003

Habari gani?

"Umoja"

In this spirit of unity, LaColis & Sharon Reed opened their home to the Arts Partners of Central Illinois to share the karamu feast and help teach new & old friends about the holiday. Distinguished Guest June Tyler lights the Umoja Candle in the Kinara, signifying the first of the 7 Principles. Garry Moore, as Facilitator, led guests through the Kwanzaa ceremonies, traditions, decorations, and greetings, and he explained the meanings of the Nguzo Saba, or 7 Guiding Principles:

Umoja – Unity
Kujichagulia – Self-Determination
Ujima – Collective Responsibility
Ujamaa – Cooperative Economics
Nia – Purpose
Kuumba – Creativity
Imani – Faith

The evening's festivities included drums, song & dance, and ended with an informal exchange of Zawadi, or "meaningful gifts." Sharon's gift was the song "Tribute" – a fitting end to a wonderful celebration with the entire community.

Kwanzaa 2003

Bay attended a ceremony to teach old and new friends about the traditions of Kwanzaa. Create texture along the edge of black cardstock background by applying ink, black embossing powder and heating. Trim edges of brown cardstock and decorate edges by applying watermark ink followed by various colors of pigment powder to create a variegated appearance. Apply same technique to small pieces of torn brown paper. Tear strips of brown cardstock. Cut horizontal slits along left side of brown paper; weave torn strips through slits. Attach brown cardstock over black with red brads. Create Kwanzaa symbols with pigment pen and red embossing powder. Print journaling on a transparency and layer on brown. Mat photos with various colors of cardstock and adhere to design.

Bay Loftis, Philadelphia, Tennessee

Supplies: Pigment powder and watermark ink (Ranger); black and brown cardstocks; red and black embossing powders; transparency; brads

Facts & Legends:

Nigerian-native Dr. Maulana Karenga, a professor at UCLA in 1966, found it difficult to celebrate American winter holidays that were specific to American cultural traditions, religions or ethnic backgrounds. As a result, Karenga invented Kwanzaa—an American celebration based on African traditions. Seven candles are lit to represent Kwanzaa's principles: unity, self-determination, collective work and responsibility, cooperative economics, purpose, creativity and faith.

Try This:

Write or type the names of Kwanzaa's seven principles on long, thin strips of paper. Decorate each to resemble a candle and include them on a layout.

Christmas

Believe

Lynette captured the moment when Santa asked her son what he wanted for Christmas and made it the focal point of her page. Trim edges of patterned paper and layer on tan paper. Mat photo on red cardstock and patterned paper; tear one side of patterned paper. Apply rub-on word along torn edge. Set large eyelets at the top and bottom of one side and thread ribbon through. Cut tag shape using a template and layer with mesh, patterned paper, and Santa image printed from the Internet. Tie tag to ribbon with fibers. Mat vellum stickers with red and tan and place below photo.

Lynette Daniel, Broken Arrow, Oklahoma

Supplies: Patterned paper (Brother Sister Designs); ribbon (Lyons Co.); fibers (EK Success); tag template (Deluxe Designs); rub-on word (Making Memories); vellum stickers (Printworks); tan and burgundy papers; mesh; eyelets

Supplies: Red, black, white and corrugated green cardstocks (DMD); metal letter charm (Making Memories); word cut-outs (7 Gypsies); hinges (Scrapworks); ribbon (Impress Rubber Stamps); acrylic charm (KI Memories); T-pin; sheet music; tag

I Think I See Santa

To document the first year her daughter understood Christmas, Peggy took a photo of her waiting for Santa to come down the chimney. Photocopy sheet music and adhere to red cardstock background. Print title vertically on white cardstock, trim into thin strip and mount to red. Tear a piece of black cardstock and layer over music. Wrap green corrugated cardstock with black gingham ribbon; accent ribbon with metal letter charm, hinges and word cut-outs. Mount journaling on tag and accent with a T-pin. Using image-editing software, manipulate date to print in white on photo. Print photo in black-and-white and highlight photo with red chalk. Mount photo on black cardstock and adorn with acrylic charm.

Peggy Manrique, Manchester Center, Vermont

A Visit With Santa

The colors of Kristen's daughters' dresses inspired the colors for her layout. Cut strip of metallic paper and mount on patterned background. Cut out title letters with a craft knife and adhere to metallic strip. Create round tags using a template; accent with holly punches and beads. Double mat one photo and wrap with fibers and tag. Cut out remainder of title with a craft knife from metallic paper and adhere to the bottom of the page. Mat other photos for second page; punch holes into one mat and through background to thread fibers. Print names on vellum and accent with punched star shapes; layer over last photo.

Kristen Swain, Bear, Delaware

Supplies: Burgundy patterned paper (Karen Foster Design); metallic paper (Paper Adventures); fibers (EK Success); tag template (Deluxe Designs); lettering template (Scrap Pagerz); holly punch (Emagination Crafts); star punch (EK Success); vellum

Believe

Vintage-style stickers give Tristann's page a textured look. Place border sticker through center of patterned paper. Add ribbon at center and bottom of page. Attach ribbon charm at bottom and apply vintage-style stickers. Layer "Believe" die cut along center ribbon. Mat photo on torn mulberry page and adhere to page.

Tristann Graves, Vancouver, Washington

Supplies: Patterned paper and Christmas stickers (Karen Foster Design); laser die-cut word (Sarah Heidt Photo Craft); ribbon charm (Making Memories); red mulberry paper; ribbon

Our Tree Is Adorned

Doris focuses on the significance of her Christmas ornaments by including each on a digitally created tag. Using image-editing software, enlarge digital photo of Christmas tree to serve as a page background. Draw a rectangle for "tag" and delete a space for photo; duplicate tag multiple times and insert photos in open spaces. Apply different colors and patterns to each tag. Import and size tree clip art and arrange with tags on background. For "vellum" journaling block, draw a text box, create layer, fill with color and adjust opacity so background shows through; type text inside.

Doris Castle, Fonda, New York

Supplies: Image-editing software (Adobe Photoshop); clip art

Santa and Me

Pam designed this layout to highlight the only photo she has of herself with Santa Claus. Embellish green cardstock by using a blow pen to splatter ink across background. Tear patterned paper, apply ink and adhere to green cardstock. Tear handmade red paper and accent with custom-printed twill tape; attach with brads. Print journaling on transparency. Mat photo in original paper frame with green cardstock. Scan "Santa and Me" design from back of original frame and print on tag. Accent tag with fibers.

Pam Sivage, Georgetown, Texas

Supplies: Patterned paper (Provo Craft); fibers (Fibers by the Yard); blow pen; green cardstock; red handmade paper; stamping ink; brads; tag; transparency; twill tape

A Gift That Keeps on Giving

Melodee's layout documents the story behind a special blanket given to her by her grandmother. Print title on patterned paper, tear and ink edges and apply to tan cardstock. Mat "A" sticker with green and position next to title. Tear and ink the edges of other patterned papers and cover background. Mat larger photo on green cardstock, ink edges and tear along one side. Using template, form pocket from patterned paper, ink edges and adorn with stickers, stamps and fibers. Print journaling on patterned paper, cut into tag shape, apply gold clip and slip into pocket. Crop other photos to fit in pocket. Create tag from patterned paper, ink edges, stamp date and add fibers. Accent layout with gold conchos.

Melodee Langworthy, Rockford, Michigan

Supplies: Patterned papers and stickers (Magenta); green textured cardstock (Bazzill); number stamps (Wordsworth); pocket template (Deluxe Designs); gold conchos and clip (Scrapworks); fibers (www.mydaughterswish.com); stamping inks

1954

Mylar wrapping paper adds color and holiday spirit to Sherry's heritage photograph. Cut wrapping paper and place along bottom of black cardstock background. Line top edge with fibers and layer with ornament punches. Cut tag from gold, layer with red and accent with metal numbers, label holder, brads, fibers and journaling printed on vellum. Mat photo with black, gold and red cardstocks. Mount metal words with green brads.

Sherry Laffoon, Modesto, California

Supplies: Ornament punch (Emagination Crafts); metal words (DieCuts with a View); metal numbers and label holder (Making Memories); black, red and gold cardstocks; wrapping paper; vellum; brads

Naughty or Nice

While Peggy and her friend decorated for Christmas, her friend's son was anything but helpful. Photos of the boy with different expressions sparked her page theme. Print words in various fonts on white cardstock. Trim red patterned paper and adhere to background. Use image-editing software to adjust color in photos, print out, mat on white and place over red. Stamp words with red ink on white twill tape and adhere to photos. Accent photos with ribbon, brads, metal letters and photo anchors. Print words on twill tape; attach some to page with staples and trim others to fit in label holders. Line bottom of page with ribbon and attach label holders and metal accent.

Peggy Roarty, Council Bluffs, Iowa

Supplies: White and black textured cardstocks (Bazzill); red patterned paper (K & Company); letter stamps (PSX Design); metal accents, photo anchors, label holders and staples (Making Memories); image-editing software; stamping ink; brads; ribbon

Christmas Wishes

Vonda used a library card as a creative way to remember her boys' Christmas wishes. Layer strips of patterned paper and green and gray cardstocks over brown paper. Attach photo with string by poking holes in the corners of the photo and the background. To embellish library card, ink edges, stamp words and add tree cut from patterned paper. Paint envelope and stitch on metal accent. Stamp title on green, cut out, ink edges and accent with star cut-outs.

Vonda Kirkpatrick, Wenatchee, Washington

Supplies: Patterned paper (Provo Craft); Santa charm (memoriesoftherabbit.com); letter stamps (Hero Arts); red acrylic paint (Delta); embroidery floss; tan, green and gray cardstocks; stamping ink; black pen; library card and pocket

Christmas Wish List

Sarah snapped these pictures of her son while asking him the top five things he wanted Santa to bring. Ink edges of gold patterned paper and layer on black cardstock. Add piece of script paper. Adhere two photos, overlapping slightly. Cut strip of red cardstock, ink edges and secure with brads. Layer cropped photo on top of red strip. Create journaling strips with a label maker and randomly place throughout design. Stamp the word "top" with letter stamps at top of page. Stamp "wish" and "5" on cream cardstock, cut apart and ink edges.

Sarah Klemish, Midland, Michigan

Supplies: Patterned papers (7 Gypsies); letter stamps (PSX Design); date stamp (Making Memories); label maker (Dymo); stamping ink; black and red cardstocks; brads

Believe

Tarri captured her children's wish list by incorporating their own handwriting. Layer striped paper on bottom half of patterned paper. Cut thin strip of rust paper and adhere where patterns meet. Cover each edge with a piece of fiber. Layer photos on background and add metal corner accents at opposite sides. Age preprinted title with sandpaper and attach to patterned and rust papers with square nails. Ink edges. Stitch along edges of rust paper for journaling block. Roll the top and bottom edges and tie with embroidery floss. Apply rub-on word to bottom of page.

Tarri Botwinski, Grand Rapids, Michigan

Supplies: Patterned paper, preprinted title and nails (Chatterbox); metal corner accents and rub-on word (Making Memories); fibers (Fibers by the Yard); embroidery floss; stamping ink; rust paper; black pen

Tree Farm

A trip to the tree farm on a freezing cold day meant hayrides, hay tunnels and hot cocoa for the Bruner family. Tear strips of white paper and layer on blue patterned paper. Cut triangles from green cardstock, outline with a metallic pen, wrap with fibers and accent with spiral clips. Arrange triangles in tree shape and cut brown rectangle for trunk. Punch circles out of blue cardstock and adhere metal letters. Outline circles with a metallic pen. Weave fiber through metal letters and adhere to page. Place photos on page, cropping around tree as needed. Print journaling, mat on blue, add eyelets and fibers.

Melanie Bruner, Knoxville, Tennessee

Supplies: Patterned paper (Close To My Heart); eyelets, metal letters and spiral clips (Making Memories); fibers; blue, white, green and brown cardstocks; circle punch; silver pen

Trim the Tree

Briana balanced a photo of her brightly lit Christmas tree with a simple, whitewashed background. Mat photo on gray paper and place on patterned paper. Print journaling on patterned paper, mat on gray and accent with snowflakes and decorative button word. Cut a 2" piece of patterned paper, mat on gray and place at top of page. Create title using letter stickers, die-cut letters and tree accent.

Briana Fisher, Milford, Michigan

Supplies: Patterned and gray papers (Mustard Moon); buttons (Jesse James); letter die cuts (Sizzix); letter stickers (Making Memories)

The Anatomy of a Tree

Ruth recorded bits of history associated with her family's tree. Layer strips of patterned paper on brown cardstock. Punch snowflakes and layer along top and bottom. Using a sewing machine, stitch two lines down the center of the snowflakes. Create an oversized mat for photos and cut triangles to act as photo corners from brown paper. Write captions on brown paper squares and place around pictures. Create title using punches, stickers, metal accents and label holder attached with brads.

Ruth De Fauw, Woodstock, Ontario, Canada

Supplies: Brown textured cardstock (Bazzill); patterned papers (Karen Foster Design); snowflake punch, postage stamp punch and round letter stickers (EK Success); letter stickers (Chatterbox); metal accents (Making Memories); label holder (www.twopeasinabucket.com); black pen; square punch

Teamwork

It takes a team of people to put the Christmas tree together in the Davenport home. Crop and mat photos on green cardstock and adhere to lighter green background. Using letter stamps and green metallic ink, stamp names on vellum, trim and adhere to pictures. Accent with thin strips of cardstock and stamp title with alphabet stamps.

Terri Davenport, Toledo, Ohio

Supplies: Letter stamps (All Night Media); green cardstocks; vellum; stamping ink

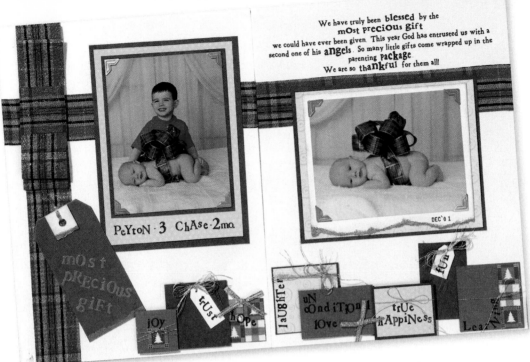

We have truly been **blessed** by the **mOst precious gift** we could have ever been given. This year God has entrusted us with a second one of his **angels**. So many little gifts come wrapped up in the parenting **package**. We are so **thankful** for them all!

Most Precious Gift

Supplies: Patterned papers (Lasting Impressions, Hot Off The Press, Making Memories); letter stamps (Missing Link); photo corners (Canson); embroidery floss; bows; white and green cardstocks; stamping ink; embossing powder; date stamp; foam tape; ribbon; tag

Amy made tiny gift boxes from paper and stamped words describing the most important gifts of the season on each. Print journaling on white cardstock background and adhere plaid ribbon horizontally and vertically. Attach gold photo corners to photos and mat on green papers. For one photo mat, tear bottom edge and heat set with gold embossing powder. Cut solid and patterned papers into squares to create gift boxes. Stamp words on squares and accent with gold ribbon. Stamp title on tag and emboss with gold powder, including bottom edge.

Amy Warren, Tyler, Texas
Photos: Cherished Memories, Tyler, Texas

Holiday Greetings

Karen created a layout using a picture included with her Christmas card. Layer patterned paper on green cardstock. Cut thin strip of patterned paper for bottom of page. Print title on patterned paper, cut apart and mount on white cardstock; adhere using foam tape. Using an envelope template, create envelope from crumpled and ironed paper, accent with punch shapes, spiral clips, eyelets and fibers. Mat photo on green cardstock with gold photo corners and layer over envelope. Create bottom border using square punches, eyelets and fibers. Insert names and date in label holder and attach to page with brads.

Karen Robinson, Cumberland, Rhode Island

Supplies: Patterned paper (Mustard Moon); circle clips (www.memoriesoftherabbit.com); fern punch (Punch Bunch); envelope template (Deluxe Designs); fibers (Kreinik); label holder; eyelets; green and cream cardstocks

Don't Tell Santa

An attempt to a take a holiday photo of all the grandkids resulted in humorous photos. Layer patterned paper on red cardstock. Tear another pattern and chalk the edges with red; adhere to one side of layout. Using image-editing software, alter pictures and distress the edges; mat on red cardstock and adhere to page. Cut out part of title with a craft knife and add to tag with brad. Print journaling and other part of title on patterned paper. Mat journaling on red cardstock.

Carrie O'Donnell, Newburyport, Massachusetts

Supplies: Red textured cardstock (Bazzill); patterned papers, sticker tag and star stickers (Magenta); brad; chalk

Our Angel

Elizabeth used snapshots of her daughter in this collage that were left over from a holiday photo shoot. Place enlarged black-and-white photo on black cardstock and layer with torn pieces of patterned paper and patterned vellum. Silhouette smaller pictures and layer on enlarged photo. Crop smaller photo to fit inside metal frame. Embellish design with ribbon, charms, tag, stickers, eyelets and metal accents. Stamp words on burgundy paper and ribbon.

Elizabeth Ruuska, Rensselaer, Indiana

Supplies: Patterned papers (7 Gypsies); letter stamps (PSX Design); metal frame, letters and word (Making Memories); angel sticker (The Gifted Line); letter stickers (Colorbök); tassel (All Night Media); black and burgundy cardstocks; eyelets; conchos; charms; vellum; gingham ribbon; stamping ink

Seasons Like This

Sharon captured a variety of family holiday moments to treasure. Layer strips of green cardstock vertically and horizontally on light green cardstock. Print title words on light green cardstock, allowing words to overlap paper strips. Attach ribbon on top of strips. Write the letter O in black pen where the ribbon covers part of the letter. Trim edges of light green cardstock and mount on dark green cardstock. Mat photos on red and green, mounting one with foam tape between the mats. Print words on cardstock and punch into circles. Accent page with circles, snowflake eyelets, ribbon charms and conchos.

Sharon Whitehead, Vernon, British Columbia, Canada

Supplies: Green and red textured cardstocks (Bazzill); ribbon charms (Making Memories); conchos (Scrapworks); eyelets (www.scrapnpaper.com); ribbon; green vellum; black pen

Holiday Baking

Tina captured her own favorite part of the holiday season—baking in the kitchen. Place three photos next to each other on light brown cardstock and layer on background paper. Print words on cream paper, cut out and layer on photos. Print title and journaling on cream paper; mat on tan. Attach title to page with copper brads.

Tina Chambers, Sardinia, Ohio

Supplies: Tan, gray and cream cardstocks; brads

Cookie Creations

On three pages, Amy documented the Christmas cookie baking process from start to finish. Crop photos and mat with gold and green cardstocks; assemble on red cardstock. Scan recipe, print on gold cardstock and mat with green. Embellish pages with felt tree stickers and buttons mounted on green cardstock and outlined with a gold pen. Create title by stitching a word with embroidery floss and stamping with letter stamps.

Amy Stultz, Mooresville, Indiana

Supplies: Felt stickers (Westrim); letter stamps (PSX Design); red, green and gold cardstocks; stamping ink; gold pen; date stamp; embroidery floss

Facts & Legends:

The image of Santa Claus as a plump, jolly man with a long beard was first introduced by cartoonist Thomas Nast for a December 1862 issue of *Harper's Weekly* magazine. Nast created a variety of other Santa illustrations that helped popularize legends associated with Santa Claus today, including the notion that Santa has a book of names of good and bad children and a workshop for making toys.

Try This:

For a vintage collage-style Christmas page, include a variety of early Santa Claus images, such as Thomas Nast's drawings for *Harper's Weekly* and Haddon Sundblom's depictions of Santa from early Coca-Cola advertisements. Search the Internet for a variety of examples or look for reproduced images on calendars, cards, etc.

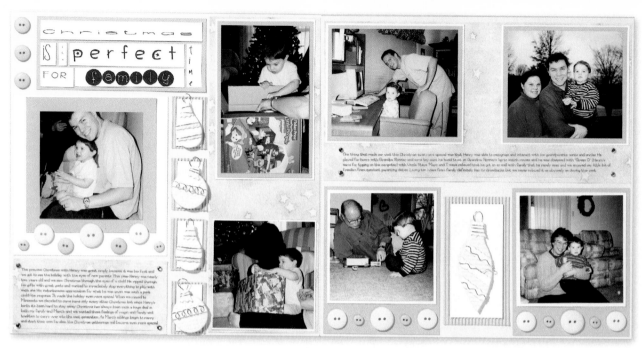

Christmas Is the Perfect Time for Family

Inspired by the color scheme of her 3-D ornament stickers, Michele created a layout to complement them. Layer sections of patterned paper on cream cardstock. Mat photos on tan and white cardstocks and place across layout. Accent select photo mats with buttons. Place 3-D stickers on white paper and corrugated cardstock and place between photos. Print journaling on vellum and attach to patterned paper with gold brads. Print title on white paper, cut words apart and piece together on tan cardstock.

Michele Skinner, Minneapolis, Minnesota

Supplies: Patterned paper (Creative Imaginations); 3-D ornament stickers (Westrim); buttons (Making Memories); tan, cream, white and corrugated cardstocks; brads

Our Christmas

Valerie instills the true meaning of Christmas by recording values of the season. Layer patterned paper on green paper background. Mat photo on tan cardstock and trim with lace, fabric, and buttons. Embellish the bottom portion with premade accents matted on brown. Print words on vellum, tear out and adhere over embellishments with eyelets. Create title using letter stickers and a tag embellished with letter stamps, patterned paper, button and premade accent.

Valerie Barton, Flowood, Mississippi

Supplies: Patterned paper and premade accents (Design Originals); letter stickers (EK Success); letter stamps (All Night Media); green paper; vellum; eyelets; fabric; lace; buttons

December 30, 2002
Stu & Julie's House

Cousins Nine

Cousins Nine

Katie shares personality descriptions of all nine cousins in her family, including some of their favorite things. Mat enlarged photo on gold cardstock and cut letters using a template for the title. Cut miniature tags from various colors of cardstock and embellish with star eyelets and embroidery floss. Print journaling in columns on tan cardstock, leaving spaces for tags. Crop photos and mat on tags; adhere within journaling.

Katie Swanson, South Milwaukee, Wisconsin

Supplies: Lettering template (Cock-A-Doodle Design); embroidery floss; star eyelets; burgundy, gold, tan and green cardstocks

Megan is a fine little artist and she also plays piano. Recently, we've learned she is quite athletic as she excelled so well on her fifth grade basketball team that she played with sixth and seventh graders in the recreation department league. She likes to play video games and also really enjoys the Harry Potter series of books. She is also interested in learning about Egypt. She's always had a loving and generous spirit.

Hannah plays the piano, too. She has a timeless beauty. She's got hair, eyes, skin, and a perfect mouth that women pay fortunes to try and get artificially. She's always been interested in horses and started taking riding lessons last fall. When she comes over to visit us, she likes to make scrapbook pages with me and create Play-Doh art. She is in second grade this year.

Michalia is another very artistic little girl. She enjoys working with crayons, markers, and paint. She sings like a bird and is quite good at that, also. When she comes over to our house, she always seems to be dancing, too! She also has a stubborn independent streak in her. And, she just loves to mother and baby her precious cousin McCoy who she dotes over like he's her son. Michalia is in kindergarten this year.

Stuart is one of the most academically gifted children I've ever met. He devours books, especially J.K. Rowling's "Harry Potter" series. (Like myself, he is eagerly awaiting the fifth installment.) This year, he began his career in Little League baseball. He also enjoys being in his little Cub Scout den. He's in second grade this year. When he gets together with McCoy, they wrestle like tiger cubs.

Natalie is another artistic cousin. She is just as academically gifted as her brother Stuart and loves to belt out a tune and dance like her cousin Michalia. She's got a mean streak in her, though, and is capable of inflicting severe bodily harm on her older brother when provoked. (Poor Stuart!) At our house, however, she's always pure angel. Go figure. She is in kindergarten this year.

Ted is also exceptionally bright – both in mind and in spirit. His speech has always been advanced for his age. He loves all animals. He's especially fond of attending his pre-school classes because he just can't get enough of learning about absolutely everything. He's also a goof like his cousin McCoy who he just so happens to look a lot like.

McCoy loves all things round – balls and wheels, that is! He loves cars, motorcycles, trucks, scooters, and skateboards. He loves many sports with balls – football, basketball, and soccer – but he also loves to swim. He loves to be goofy enough for his cousins and classmates to belly laugh out loud at his antics. He is a very picky eater and prefers to eat plain pasta at every meal. He is in kindergarten this year.

Sophie loves to draw with crayons and markers on paper, tables, walls, clothes and her own little body. She loves her books, too – especially the ones about her favorite character, "Dora the Explorer." She's often found singing – she really loves "Twinkle, Twinkle Little Star," "The ABC Song," and "The Wheels on the Bus." She also likes to shake her little booty!

At the ripe age of one, Ava has already developed a love of books. She is a peaceful child who can be leery when she's first presented with a large group of unfamiliar faces. But she warms up really fast into a sweet and loving girl – especially if you share food with her! She has a bit more of a demure personality than most of the cousins. Her looks and personality are the most like Hannah's

H Is for Home

Hilary created a spread to showcase her family's treasured nativity decorations. Mat photo with large green mat and adhere to tan background. Assemble tree embellishment from papers, jump rings and star punch and adhere to mat with fiber. Cut small squares of various patterned papers and adhere buttons with raffia for embellishment. Make title out of letter stickers mounted on cardstock. Create photo mosaic by cutting various pictures into 1" squares and adhering them next to each other on green cardstock; accent with fiber.

Hilary Erickson, Santa Clara, California

Supplies: Green patterned papers (used on tree, Close To My Heart); other patterned papers (source unknown); letter stickers (source unknown); buttons; star punch; jump rings; raffia; tan, green, white and yellow cardstocks

...to Be a Child?

Kara uses a preprinted quote to capture the essence of childhood. Tear patterned paper; chalk the edges and adhere to top and bottom of green patterned paper. Distress premade frame with sandpaper, layer over photo and accent with premade bow. Apply 3-D heart stickers and embellish with metallic rub-ons. Tear edges of vellum quote and place over patterned paper; tear edges and rub with metallic rub-ons.

Kara Swink, Houston, Texas

Supplies: Music patterned paper (Hot Off The Press); green patterned paper (Wright Designs); premade frame and bow (My Mind's Eye); 3-D heart stickers (EK Success); vellum quote (Memories Complete); chalk; metallic rub-ons

Sights of Christmas

The sights and sounds of Christmas are things that Tina would like her family to always remember. Crop photos and create a photo montage on red cardstock. Punch squares from green and white and write numbers on each. Print title on white cardstock and double mat with green cardstock and patterned paper; adhere with brads. Create right page by layering patterned paper on red cardstock and adhering a premade tree embellishment. Print journaling on white paper and mat on green. Print reduced images of CD covers, mat on green cardstock and attach with brads.

Tina Chambers, Sardinia, Ohio

Supplies: Patterned paper (Provo Craft); premade tree embellishment (Ivy Cottage Creations); white, burgundy and green cardstocks; brads; black pen

A Nelson Family Tradition

Kate used scraps of wrapping paper to construct a multi-colored tree accent. Layer burgundy cardstock on green plaid paper. Tear green speckled paper diagonally and place in lower lefthand corner. Cut wrapping paper to form a tree and star shapes; mount on cream cardstock and outline with a black pen. Mat photo and journaling on green cardstock and adhere to page.

Kate Nelson, Fountain, Colorado

Supplies: Patterned papers (Bo-Bunny Press, Provo Craft); burgundy and green cardstocks; black pen; wrapping papers

Each year we add new ornaments to our family's Christmas tree--one that is personally selected by each member of the family. Our tree has new and richer meaning for us since each ornament tells a story and reflects the member of the family who selected it that year.

Supplies: Patterned paper (Brother Sister Designs); fibers (Fibers by the Yard); tan, green and cream cardstocks; eyelets; tissue paper; stamping ink; craft foam; ribbon; velvet

Check This Out

Inspired by the mess made on Christmas morning, Susan created an "exploded" Santa bag. Tear patterned paper diagonally and mount in opposite corners of tan background. Ink all edges of paper. Mat photos on cream and green cardstocks and place on pages. Cut title from red cardstock with a craft knife. Print journaling on patterned paper, tear edges and attach with eyelets. Wrap red velvet around craft foam and tie with ribbon to make Santa bag. Collage another tag with scraps of velvet and crumpled paper. Attach journaled tags to both bags with eyelets.

Susan Stringfellow, Cypress, Texas

Facts & Legends:

The legend of Santa Claus is based on the generous spirit of a man named Nicholas, born around 275 A.D. in Lycia (now Turkey). Nicholas' wealthy parents died of the plague when he was just a boy. Under the care of his uncle, a bishop, Nicholas became a priest at age 19, and later a bishop himself. He was well known for giving gifts and food to the needy, and many legends exist about miracles Nicholas performed during his lifetime. After his death on December 6, 343, Catholics declared him a saint and began to celebrate St. Nicholas Day with a feast. By the 12th century, children would set out shoes, socks and paper boats to be filled with gifts from "St. Nicholas" on the night before December 6. After the Reformation, Protestants did not celebrate St. Nicholas Day, but many wanted to keep the traditions alive. People started to observe St. Nicholas traditions on December 25, the day for celebrating the birth of Jesus. St. Nicholas became known as Father Christmas by the English, Pere Nöel by the French, Weihnachtmann (Christmas man) by the Germans and Sinterklaas by the Dutch. Many historians believe that mispronunciations of Sinterklaas eventually gave rise to the name "Santa Claus" used in America.

Try This:

Using a variety of fonts, type the names given to Santa Claus in other countries. Repeat the names many times and print on cardstock or a transparency as a decorative border or background design.

Christmas 2003

Doris included a blurred photo on this layout for a soft effect and to capture the glow of the tree. With image-editing software, enlarge photo of tree and layer with red pattern. Draw box and fill with color for "photo mats." For torn photo mat, draw jagged lines around a box, then draw folds and fill with gradient and texture. Draw stitching and apply wave filter for a realistic look. For journaling background, draw a box, fill with white, decrease opacity and add texture using the layer styles box. Type title in text box. Give title, photo frame and heart accent a metallic look by applying a preset layer style.

Doris Castle, Fonda, New York

Supplies: Image-editing software (Adobe Photoshop)

What a Cool Yule

Deda's journaling was inspired by a Hanes underwear commercial featuring Michael Jordan. Layer patterned paper on red cardstock. Mat photo on white, green and red cardstocks; embellish mats with fibers, glitter stickers and metal letters. For title letters, apply white ink, glitter and embossing powder to metal letters and paper circles. Adhere letters to circles and attach circles to string with bits of gray paper. Print journaling; tear and chalk edges. Stamp date, mat, add glitter and hang from sticker with fiber.

Deda Chase, Tulsa, Oklahoma

Supplies: Patterned paper (Hot Off The Press); circle template (Provo Craft); metal accents, date stamp (Making Memories); 3-D poinsettia stickers (EK Success); metal letters (DieCuts with a View); red, green and white cardstocks; stamping ink; embossing powder, glitter; fibers; chalk

Family Ties

father gave me the greatest gift anyone could give
another person... he believed in me.

Father's Day
2003

MOTHER'S 2003
DAY

My heart
is FULL
on this
beautiful
day with my
beautiful
KIDS

a mother's love
is

RYAN MOMMY LAUREN

Spring HOLIDAYS

Tiny buds on tree branches, moist green grass and baby birds stretching open-mouthed to the sky remind us that winter is over and another season of life has begun. Spring holiday pages overflow with newness in a variety of ways: There's the celebration of new life at Easter, the cleansing of the home at Passover, renewed appreciation for our parents on Mother's Day and Father's Day and a fresh understanding of those who have fought for our country on Memorial Day. Whichever holidays you wish to include in your albums this spring, this chapter will provide a variety of fresh perspectives.

Find Page Ideas For...

Passover

Debra included information from the Haggadah, the guidebook used during the Passover Seder, on her spread. Mat photos on patterned paper and green cardstocks and place on patterned background paper. Print journaling on colored vellum and attach to metallic and patterned papers with rivets. Print title on colored vellum and heat emboss copper powder over letters. Mat on patterned and metallic papers and accent with fibers. Attach vellum envelope and accent with fiber. For right page, adhere strip of brown patterned paper to background. Adhere wine goblet die cut to vellum and layer over brown. Print journaling on vellum and attach over die cut with rivets. Triple mat other photos.

Debra Hendren, Royal Oak, Michigan

Supplies: Patterned papers (Karen Foster Design); embossing powder (Stampendous); fibers (EK Success); wine goblet die cut (Deluxe Designs); green cardstock; metallic paper; eyelets; rivets; stamping ink

Passover

Supplies: Fibers and eyelets (Making Memories); patterned paper (Provo Craft); image-editing software (Adobe Photoshop); silver Passover charms (source unknown); blue, green, orange and white cardstocks

Passover Seder

Kelly used vibrant colors to document a kid-friendly Seder she had with two other families. Cut many thin strips of colored cardstocks; layer over white background. Crop photos and mat with colored cardstocks and patterned paper. Scan photo of Seder plate and matzo, enlarge and change to "pencil lines" using image-editing software. Lighten images, print on vellum, cut out and accent with colored pencils. Punch paper circles in different sizes and arrange across spread. Attach charms to paper circles and squares and tie onto fibers. Set eyelets on each page, thread fibers through and tape to backs of pages. Print title and silhouette each letter. Print journaling on vellum, trim and adhere to layout.

Kelly Angard, Highlands Ranch, Colorado

Facts & Legends:

Part of preparing the home for the Passover season includes removing all chametz from the house—any food that has risen or contains yeast. Foods that touch chametz also should be removed. This symbolizes freshness and new beginnings.

Try This:

To illustrate the cleansing of the home during Passover, photograph bread, cake, cookies and other items in a group. Stamp and heat emboss the words "Do Not Use" on a transparency and lay it over the photo on a page.

Easter

DYEING EGGS

Supplies: Patterned paper
(Doodlebug Design); lettering
template (Scrap Pagerz);
balloon punch (Marvy);
paper crimper (Paper
Adventures); blue, white and
tan papers; stapler; chalk;
white marker

Easter 2003- Egg dyeing was a treat this year. The dye kit was a rub on type. We took droppers of color and a plastic bag and put the egg in and smushed the color over the egg. It was lots of fun and easy to do for the girls. The clean up was easy too, no dishes to do! Even though we don't do anything much with the eggs. The tradition of doing them and the minimal cost makes it worthwhile for the memories we have created with you girls. I hope you both will remember sitting around the table with mommy and daddy and having a great time, getting messy and laughing a lot. We love you!

Dyeing Eggs

A mini album allowed Kristen to add more egg-dyeing photos. Cut strips of patterned paper and adhere over blue. Crop and adhere photos. Print journaling on white and adhere to page. Cut thin strips of cream paper, crimp and adhere to page in two clumps. Use template to cut title letters and adhere at top. Use a balloon punch to create eggs and cut thin strips of tan paper to make basket. Assemble pieces and adhere over other crumpled paper. Mat multiple photos, stack on top of one another and staple across top edge to create mini album.

Kristen Swain, Bear, Delaware

Easter Eggs

A single photograph served as the basis of Jennifer's computer-generated layout. With photo-editing software, create copy of digital photo and place one on top of the other. Make top copy black-and-white. With the eraser tool, erase eggs on top copy to reveal colored eggs below. Merge two photos together and enlarge image. Use paintbrush tool to make background black. Type title and journaling. Use eyedropper tool to apply exact egg colors to title letters.

Jennifer Ditterich, Chokio, Minnesota

Supplies: Image-editing software (Adobe Photoshop Elements)

EASTER Eggs

The boys loved playing with the Easter eggs this year. I hid little treats inside some of the eggs, like coins and candy, and then mixed the pile of eggs up. They had so much fun digging through the eggs to find their treasures and they laughed and giggled the whole time.

Dying Eggs

Martha used colorful round tags as a title to represent the colored eggs in the pictures. Mat photos on white cardstock and place on patterned paper background. Place letter stickers on colored circle tags; accent tags with fibers. Print journaling on vellum and place over photo.

Martha Crowther, Salem, New Hampshire

Supplies: Patterned paper (Provo Craft); fibers (Fibers by the Yard); tags (Making Memories); letter stickers (Creative Imaginations); white cardstock

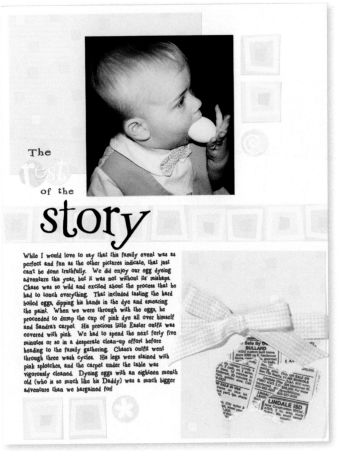

The Rest of the Story

Amy recounts the family mishaps that occurred while trying to dye Easter eggs. Print journaling on white cardstock. Cut pieces of patterned paper and arrange on page. Crop photo and layer over patterned paper. Scan and print newspaper, tear edges and place on patterned paper. Add circle and letter stickers and accent with ribbon.

Amy Warren, Tyler, Texas

Supplies: Patterned paper (KI Memories); letter and circlestickers (Creative Imaginations); white cardstock; ribbon

Egg Fight

To remedy the never-ending problem of leftover Easter eggs, the Warren family has a food fight in their back yard. For left page, adhere thin strip of blue paper to the center of patterned paper. Attach photos and stickers. For right page, print journaling on patterned paper, then tear patterned paper and place on blue cardstock. Add strip of blue paper and letter and accent stickers. Mat photo and adhere to page. Slice one photo and adhere to both sides of spread.

Amy Warren, Tyler, Texas

Supplies: Patterned paper, accent and letter stickers (Doodlebug Design); black letter stickers (Wordsworth); blue paper

Egg Hunt

Chris captured the egg-hunting process through a variety of action shots. Print journaling on green cardstock and adhere to patterned paper. Add vellum letter stickers for the title. Double mat one photo on pink and blue and place in the bottom right-hand corner. Crop other photos and adhere to layout.

Chris Douglas, East Rochester, Ohio

Supplies: Patterned paper (K & Company); letter stickers (Mrs. Grossman's); green, blue and pink cardstocks

Easter Egg Hunt Strategies

Pam records each child's strategy to find Easter eggs on Sunday morning. Print title and journaling on vellum and ink edges. Accent title with eyelets and fibers; curl one end of each journaling strip. Ink an additional piece of vellum and place on patterned background, layer with photo and add fibers and basket button. Attach journaling pieces with colored snaps. Create picture frames out of patterned paper, crop photos to fit inside and embellish with letter beads and buttons.

Pam Canavan, Clermont, Florida

Supplies: Patterned paper (K & Company); eyelets; snaps and fibers (Making Memories); egg and basket buttons (Jesse James); letter beads (Westrim); stamping ink; vellum

Alex

Susan's layout shows places that eggs are hidden on Easter. Cut 1½" strip of teal cardstock and mount vertically on left side of page. Layer horizontally with patterned vellum and adhere with colored brads. Mat photos on white, teal and green paper and accent with fibers. Cut thin strips of patterned vellum and adhere diagonally on left side of page. Cut name from purple cardstock using a lettering template and a craft knife. Print journaling on a transparency; apply embossing ink and powder. Heat around edges and stitch to page with fibers. Add word and letter stickers and stamped images accented with chalk.

Susan Stringfellow, Cypress, Texas

Supplies: Green patterned paper and brads (Making Memories); patterned vellum (NRN Designs); transparency; word sticker (Bo Bunny Press); letter stickers, lettering template (Wordsworth); fibers (Fibers by the Yard); stamps (PSX Design); purple and blue cardstocks; stamping ink; chalk; embossing ink

Sure Signs of Spring

Katie captures many reminders of spring: candy, green grass, flowers and a new Easter dress and hat. Print title and journaling on patterned paper, trim and adhere to green cardstock. Add photo and stickers. Cut thin strips of colored paper; place vertically along one side and layer with fibers of the same color. Adhere photos with foam tape over fibers. Create border with square-punched shapes and buttons.

Katie Nelson, Murray, Utah

Supplies: Green textured cardstock (Bazzill); yellow patterned paper (source unknown); other patterned papers (American Crafts, Pebbles); buttons (Making Memories); stickers (Colorbök); purple, orange and yellow papers; fibers; foam tape

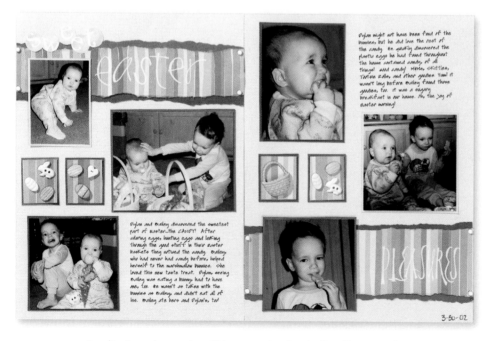

Sweet Easter

For Kelli's kids, the sweetest part of Easter is the candy. Print journaling on lavender background paper. Tear strips of purple, blue and patterned paper and attach with brads on both pages. Mat photos on various colors of cardstock and adhere to page. Create accent blocks by cutting small squares of patterned paper and cardstock and embellishing with Easter buttons. Apply letter stickers and rub-on words for title.

Kelli Lawlor, Norfolk, Virginia

Supplies: Lavender, purple and blue textured cardstocks (Bazzill); patterned paper (Scrapbook Wizard); letter stickers (Creative Imaginations); rub-on words (Making Memories); heart button (Making Memories); egg and bunny buttons (Jesse James); brads

Chocolate Bunny

Susan recounts her daughter's excitement for the treasures in her Easter basket. Trim pink patterned paper and layer on green patterned paper. Crop and mat photos on pale pink cardstock and adhere to page. Print journaling on pink paper. Cut strips of patterned vellum and place on top and bottom of page; accent with sheer ribbon. Tear heart patterned paper and place along ribbon on bottom of page. Silhouette cut illustrations from patterned paper and use as accents. Embellish with 3-D chocolate bunny sticker.

Susan Kresge, Temple Terrace, Florida

Supplies: Green patterned paper (Frances Meyer); pink patterned paper, heart patterned paper, patterned vellum (source unknown); 3-D chocolate bunny sticker (EK Success); ribbon

Easter Morning

Lynne captures the Easter morning routine enjoyed by her 16-year-old son. Layer blue paper on white cardstock. Cut curved pieces from patterned papers and white cardstock; layer on page. Create photo mat from torn pieces of patterned paper and white cardstock; accent with buttons and embroidery floss. Write journaling on strips of white cardstock and mount on torn pieces of blue paper. Attach with brads and weave fiber throughout. Write title on vellum tags and accent with fibers and buttons. Attach metal letters with brads.

Lynne Rigazio Mau, Channahon, Illinois

Supplies: Patterned papers (Mustard Moon); buttons, vellum tags, metal letters (Making Memories); fibers (Fibers by the Yard); blue and gray pens (EK Success); brads; white cardstock; blue paper; embroidery floss

Easter Memories

Mendy records her mother's decoration efforts for the grandchildren at Easter. Mat photos on patterned paper and tear along bottom edge; accent with fibers and copper brads. Frame cropped pictures with blue slide mounts. Print journaling on a transparency and place on patterned background. Create part of title using die-cut letters and patterned paper; use sticker word to finish. Attach egg dipping tool.

Mendy Douglass, Frankfort, Kentucky

Supplies: Blue/green patterned paper (Wordsworth); blue patterned paper (Paper Illuzionz); word sticker (EK Success); slide mounts (Jest Charming); letter die cuts (QuicKutz); fibers (Ties that Bind); transparency; brads; egg dipping tool

Grandma went to a lot of trouble to make Easter fun this year! she decided we would dye eggs this year, and we spent the afternoon enjoying each others company and coloring easter eggs. She made a wonderful bunny cake for dinner and mom made sure we all awoke to Easter nests filled with sugary goodness.
Easter 2003

Easter

Stacy created a page showcasing Easter spent with her daughter's great-grandmother. Adhere lace across the bottom of tan background. Tear cream paper and chalk edges for photo mats. Crumple, chalk and layer two photo mats for one photo. Embellish premade title and tags with buttons, beads, letter stickers, die cut and wire. Attach tags to page with brads. Add letter stickers to background.

Stacy Hackett, Murrieta, California

Supplies: Premade title, tags and butterfly die cut (Li'l Davis Designs); letter stickers (Creative Imaginations, Provo Craft); tan and cream cardstocks; wire; brads; fibers; pearl beads; chalk; buttons

Easter

Maegan balanced the dark backgrounds of portraits with a light, elegant design. Layer embossed and embroidered papers and stitch together with taupe embroidery floss. Mat pictures on patterned paper and brown cardstock; accent one with sheer ribbon. Hand stitch title on page with embroidery floss. Attach floss to preprinted egg accents and hang from buttons.

Maegan Hall, Virginia Beach, Virginia

Supplies: Embossed paper (K & Company); embroidered paper (Creative Imaginations); patterned paper (source unknown); preprinted egg accents (EK Success); brown cardstock; ribbon; embroidery floss; buttons

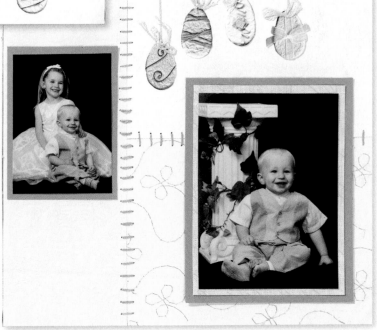

Facts & Legends:

For Christians, Easter celebrates the resurrection of Jesus, who died to forgive the sins of humankind. Before Jesus' time on Earth, eggs had long served as a symbol of new life and were used in spring festivals by many different cultures. Due to their connection to new life, eggs remained a symbol of Easter for many Christians. Even Christian legends about coloring eggs developed. One legend says that an egg merchant, Simon of Cyrene, put down his basket of eggs in order to carry Jesus' cross. When he went back for his basket, all the eggs were colored. Another story suggests that eggs were originally dyed red to represent Jesus' blood.

Try This:

To subtly represent the egg and the spirit of new life on your next Easter layout, incorporate oval shapes in your page design. Repeat the shape across the background in a random fashion, using one oval for journaling. Allow the shape to bleed off the edges of your page for added interest.

First Easter Dress

Christina's daughter's Easter dress inspired her color scheme. Tear strips of embossed vellum and place along top and side of purple cardstock background. Adhere photos, placing some in premade frames. Attach premade border along bottom. Print journaling on vellum and adhere to page. Cut flowers from patterned paper and vellum to use as accents throughout. Stitch flowers with embroidery floss. Cut part of title from purple cardstock cut using a craft knife; mount letters on vellum printed with remainder of title. Place headband in memorabilia holder and attach to page. Accent with tag.

Christina Gibson, Jonesboro, Arkansas

Supplies: Patterned paper, vellum, premade frames and borders (K & Company); tag (Making Memories); number stickers (Provo Craft); memorabilia keeper (C-Thru Ruler); embroidery floss

Easter

Carolyn created a page recalling what it was like to spend time with extended family when she was younger. Trim patterned paper and layer on wine cardstock. Add strip of pink cardstock on left side. Cover strip with green ribbon. Punch squares and add letter stickers to each square for title; mount over ribbon. Trim one photo and pink cardstock with decorative scissors. Mat photo on pink and green. Apply stickers to green rectangle and mat on deckle-cut pink and wine cardstocks. Frame other photo with premade frame and ribbon; mat on pink. Print journaling on pink paper and mat on wine cardstock. Embellish page with 3-D and button stickers.

Carolyn Cleveland, Maysville, Georgia

Supplies: Patterned paper (Mustard Moon); premade frame, ribbon and button cutouts (My Mind's Eye); 3-D stickers (EK Success); letter stickers (Club Scrap); green, pink and wine cardstocks; decorative scissors

Easter Bonnet

Mary-Catherine created a layout inspired by the bonnet her mother made for her daughter's first Easter. Tear nursery rhyme and definition patterned papers and layer over pink patterned paper. Enlarge photo and adhere to page; layer with sewing patterned tissue paper. Crop photos to fit in small square tags. Stamp title letters on pink cardstock, heat set with black embossing powder and cut out. Accent page with metal label holder, stick pins and stamped tag adorned with gingham ribbon.

Mary-Catherine Kropinski
Maple Ridge, British Columbia, Canada

Supplies: Nursery rhyme and pink patterned papers (Rusty Pickle); definition and patterned tissue papers (7 Gypsies); letter stamps (PSX Design, Wordsworth); metal label holder, stick pin, vellum tags and ribbon (Making Memories); pink cardstock; embossing powder; stamping ink

He is Risen

Pamela used photos of church banners to illustrate her beliefs and religious traditions surrounding Easter. Trim metallic gold and cream papers; layer over purple cardstock. Adhere gold thread along the top and bottom edges. Crop picture into a mosaic and layer on cream, gold and purple. Print journaling on vellum. Cut words from photograph with a craft knife to create title. Create the rest of title with die cut letters. Accent with silhouetted piece of photo.

Pamela James, Ventura, California

Supplies: Gold metallic cardstock (source unknown); cream metallic cardstock (Club Scrap); letter die cuts (Sizzix); purple cardstock; gold thread

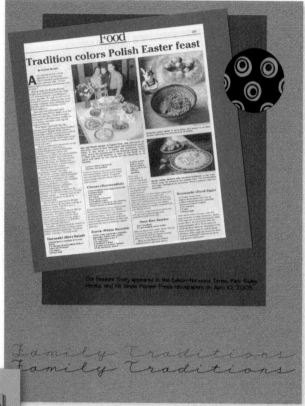

Polish Easter Traditions

Ann and her husband cherish and preserve their Polish heritage. On these computer-generated layouts, she documents symbolic foods included in her Easter dinner and baskets. Open photo files on the computer. Draw boxes for page backgrounds using image-editing software; fill in background color using the eyedropper tool. Move photos over backgrounds. Draw other boxes and fill with colors and patterns as desired. For blue circle pattern shown on two pages above, scan design from plate and import onto layout. Using the text tool, create text boxes and type journaling.

Ann Hetzel Gunkel, Chicago, Illinois

Supplies: Image editing software (Adobe Photoshop)

Easter

To preserve a tradition from their cultural heritage, Oksanna's family enjoys playing a game from the Ukraine developed long ago. Print journaling on vellum and tear along one side. Machine stitch vellum to patterned background paper. Add sparkle spray to background. Double mat one photo and adhere all to page. Apply dimensional paint around matted photo. Punch border from white cardstock. Create title by stamping into clay and poking holes in each side. Attach clay over vellum with eyelets and fibers. Accent vellum with tiny glass marbles. Apply texture stamp and pink stamping ink to slide mount. Print additional journaling on white and use slide mount as a frame. Stamp basket on white, silhouette cut and attach to side of slide mount.

Oksanna Pope, Los Gatos, California

Supplies: Patterned paper, letter and texture stamps (PSX Design); beads, sparkle spray and dimensional paint (Duncan); slide mount (Design Originals); clay (Provo Craft); fibers (EK Success); border punch (Fiskars); white and pink cardstocks; eyelets; stamping ink

Babka

At Easter, each member of Oksanna's family takes turns decorating traditional Ukrainian bread with icing. Apply sparkle spray to patterned paper background. Mount photos on blue cardstock and adhere to patterned paper. Cut two strips of cardstock with decorative scissors, weave strips together and adhere to one photo mat. Punch circles, stamp letters on each and adhere over one photo with foam tape. Enlarge photo of bread, silhouette cut and add letters with dimensional paint. Layer with letters cut from template. Print journaling on cardstock, mat and arrange across bottom. Accent with pink beads.

Oksanna Pope, Los Gatos, California

Supplies: Patterned papers (Design Originals); sparkle spray, dimensional paint and beads (Duncan); texture stamp, letter stamps (PSX Design); circle punch, foam tape (All Night Media); letter templates (Accu-Cut, C-Thru Ruler); decorative scissors (Fiskars); blue, pink and cream cardstocks; stamping inks

Mother's Day

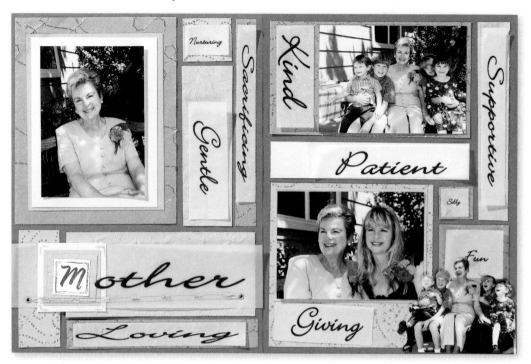

Supplies: Textured papers (Provo Craft); gray cardstock and cream metallic papers (DMD); sparkle spray and fabric paint (Duncan); letter stamps (All Night Media); fibers (EK Success); eyelets; vellum

Mother

Oksanna included qualities her mother possesses on this spread. Cut textured papers in rectangles and squares; assemble on gray cardstock background sprayed with sparkle spray. Crop and mat photos to fit over larger rectangles. Print words on vellum, cut into strips and layer over paper. Accent title strip with eyelets, fibers, cardstock squares, stamped letter and fabric paint. Silhouette cut one picture and adhere in lower right corner.

Oksanna Pope, Los Gatos, California

Happy Mother's Day

Mary included a photo of her mother-in-law's favorite flower to show her appreciation on a layout. Mat photo on lavender cardstock and layer on patterned paper. Print journaling on vellum and attach with purple brads. Layer mesh, paper, beads, wire, pewter sticker, heart punch, circle clip and letter beads over lavender tag; finish tag with fibers.

Mary Litton, Holloman Air Force Base, New Mexico

Supplies: Patterned paper (Mustard Moon); heart punch (EK Success); stickers, fibers, letter beads, glass beads, circle clip and brads (www.memories oftherabbit.com); mesh (Magic Mesh); lavender cardstock; vellum; wire

First Mother's Day

Stacy created a layout describing her first Mother's Day experience while pregnant. Over green cardstock background, layer strips of yellow cardstock and patterned papers; accent with machine stitching. Crop and mat photo on cream and pink cardstocks and adhere to page. Print journaling on cream cardstock and accent with lace flowers. Cut tags from patterned paper, accordion-fold and stitch to page. Frame cropped photo with patterned paper, stitch edges and layer over tags. Create title with letter stamps and letter page pebbles.

Stacy Yoder, Yucaipa, California

Supplies: Patterned papers (7 Gypsies, Design Originals, Magenta); letter pebbles (Creative Imaginations); letter stamps (PSX Design); green and yellow cardstocks, stamping ink; chalk

My Mom…

Becoming a parent herself led Stacy to recount the circumstances surrounding her childhood. Crumple patterned papers, then flatten, sand, ink and tear edges. Adhere to green cardstock. Mat older photos on cream cardstock, ink mats and place at angles over patterned paper. Mat main photo on blue cardstock and accent with premade paper strips. Print journaling on cream cardstock; tear and ink edges. Create title with alphabet stamps and letters cut from blue cardstock with a craft knife. Accent with metal label holders, number stickers and black pen.

Stacy Yoder, Yucaipa, California

Supplies: Green textured cardstock (Bazzill); patterned papers (KI Memories, Making Memories); paper strips and letter stickers (Chatterbox); letter punch-outs (Scrapworks); letter stamps (Hero Arts, PSX Design); stamping ink; snaps (Doodlebug Design); metal label holders (Magic Scraps); foam tape

Mother's Day

Mary created a page describing the bond shared with her son. Layer pieces of patterned and embossed papers on peach cardstock. Trace papers with a gold paint pen. Mat photos with photo corners on white cardstock, tear right edges of mats and color with gold pen. For fold-out, fold white cardstock in half. Print journaling and attach to inside. Tear top edge, color with gold pen and attach journaling printed on vellum and textured paper to top flap with gold brads. Attach fold-out to page.

Mary Walby, Royal Oak, Michigan
Photos: Leo Knight Studios, Southfield, Michigan

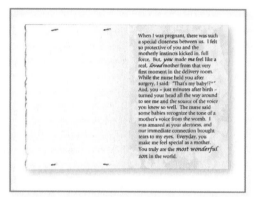

When I was pregnant, there was such a special closeness between us. I felt so protective of you and the motherly instincts kicked in, full force. But, *you* made me feel like a real, *loved* mother from that very first moment in the delivery room. While the nurse held you after surgery, I said: "That's my baby!!*" And, you – just minutes after birth – turned your head all the way around to see me and the source of the voice you knew so well. The nurse said some babies recognize the tone of a mother's voice from the womb. I was amazed at your alertness, and our immediate connection brought tears to my eyes. Everyday, you make me feel special as a mother. You truly are the *most wonderful son* in the world.

Supplies: Patterned paper, patterned vellum and word stickers (EK Success); textured flower paper (Paper Diva); gold paint pen (Marvy); brads (Doodlebug Design); photo corners (Canson); peach and white cardstocks

Facts & Legends:

Although Mother's Day did not become a national holiday in the United States until 1914, England observed an unrelated holiday called "Mothering Sunday" in the 1600s, on the 4th Sunday of Lent. On this day, young people working in other homes as domestic servants would be given the day off to return to their "mother church" and spend the day with their families. They often brought flowers, small gifts or desserts called "mothering cakes" to their mothers at this time.

Try This:

Let the English tradition of "mothering cakes" set the stage for a sweet and tasty Mother's Day page. Decorate a page with images of Mom's favorite desserts, either store-bought or homemade. Include stamped images of layer cakes, bite-sized chocolates handmade from paper, color-copied candy packaging or anything else that tempts Mom's sweet tooth. If it's a homemade dessert, add a copy of the recipe to the page.

I received the best mother's day gift ever...before I became a mother.

My parents gave me a great gift each day when I was growing up by providing me with excellent role models. Of course, at that time, I was too immature, too young and too into myself to realize that it was a gift. There were some days when I wouldn't even accept their gift, but that didn't deter them, they kept at it no matter what.

It was not until I actually became a Mother that I realized what they had done for me. Each day of James' life, I try to remember the gift and bestow it on James. Some days it is hard, but I always know that ultimately I will do the right thing for that is the best way to repay my parents for their gift.

My inspiration My parents

Best Mother's Day Gift

Pam reflected her parents as role models for this page. Print title and journaling on vellum, tear edges and apply stamping ink. Layer on patterned paper and attach with brads. Mat photo on white cardstock and ink the edges. Insert vellum words in metal label holder. Accent page with label holder and tiles.

Pam Canavan, Clermont, Florida

Supplies: Patterned paper (Creative Imaginations); tiles (Mosaic Mercantile); metal label holder (Li'l Davis Designs); vellum; stamping ink; brads

As a child, I always loved to listen to my parents tell stories of the old days back home. I could hear the same story, over and over, yet never tire of it. As I grew older, these stories accompanied other activities that I did with my mother. My mother was never one to sit idle. We did embroidery or played cards. As an adult, I looked forward to a string of days off from work, so I could go spend a few nights at home with my mum. We sat every evening together in the living room, drinking tea, knitting countless sweaters and chatting. Now, at seventy-four years of age, my mum's eyesight is failing because of cataracts and her memory is slipping away. My parents now live in the country. Since neither of us drive, getting together like before is difficult. We cannot knit or chat like we used to and I so miss it. I have realised, even more than ever, to cherish the time that we have

laura & mum

Mother's Day

LauraLinda fondly remembers times spent with her mother listening to stories, embroidering and playing cards. Tear bottom edge of patterned paper and layer on light pink cardstock. Machine stitch two rows across spread. Add border and letter stickers, faux wax seal and stamps in between rows. For left page, triple mat one photo, stitch around mat and adhere to page. Cut out letters with craft knife and add letter stickers below photo. For right side, print journaling on pink cardstock, attach photo, tear bottom edge and stitch to page. Color edges of mat with metallic rub-ons and accent with stickers and torn paper.

LauraLinda Rudy, Markham, Ontario, Canada

Supplies: patterned paper, stickers, faux wax seal (Creative Imaginations); pebble letters (Li'l Davis Designs); metallic rub-ons (Craf-T); pink cardstock; thread

Memorial Day Picnic

Brandi recorded Memorial Day by taking snapshots of friends at her church's annual picnic. Layer patterned paper on red cardstock; place rickrack over the seam. Mount three photos along red cardstock. Print names on white, cut into tag shapes and embellish with black pen, eyelets and paper yarn. Cut strips of yellow paper and mount at angles on patterned paper; layer photo on top and accent with buttons. Create the title with die-cut letters. Print journaling and embellish with black pen and red chalk.

Brandi Ginn, Lafayette, Colorado

Supplies: Patterned paper (Two Busy Moms); tag template, chalk (Deluxe Designs); buttons (Junkitz); letter die cuts (QuicKutz); paper yarn and eyelets (Making Memories); red cardstock; foam tape

Why

"Why?" was Pam's son's reaction when he saw the Vietnam Memorial, which she used as a page title. Place white tiles at the top and cropped photo at the bottom of sparkle paper. Print journaling on vellum and punch three squares along the top and bottom, aligned with tiles and photo. Adhere photo to vellum sheet, punch another square from smaller piece of vellum and layer over photo. Accent page with square tiles. Write title on white tiles.

Pam Canavan, Clermont, Florida

Supplies: Sparkle paper (Paper Adventures); tiles (EK Success); vellum; square punch; black pen

Remembering

Touched by her child's desire to remember those who have passed on, Lisa captured what was significant to her daughter. Tear and chalk the edges of vellum and attach to patterned paper with star eyelets. Mat photos on tan, red and blue cardstocks. Print journaling on tan cardstock; mat and adhere to page. Cut out title using a lettering template and accent with eyelets.

Lisa Turley, Chesapeake, Virginia

Supplies: Patterned paper (K & Company); lettering template (Scrap Pagerz); star and round eyelets (Happy Hammer); red, blue and tan cardstocks; vellum; chalk; black pen

Facts & Legends:

Originally known as Decoration Day, Memorial Day was established in 1868 to remember soldiers lost in the Civil War. President Lyndon Johnson and Congress recognized Waterloo, New York, as the birthplace of Memorial Day—its residents began decorating soldiers' graves in 1866.

Try This:

Decorate your next page of a Memorial Day get-together with Civil War images, symbols or slogans to pay tribute to the holiday's origins. Journal about when Memorial Day was established in addition to recording your personal memories of the day.

Father's Day at Ocean Shores

Andrea captured Father's Day events with black-and-white photos on a serene layout. Adhere photos to blue cardstock. Print title and journaling on light blue paper, cut apart and sand the edges. Cut border from patterned paper, sand edges and adhere to page.

Andrea Hautala, Olympia, Washington

Supplies: Patterned paper (Sonburn); blue cardstock

Family

Despite a few mishaps, Joanna and her family enjoyed their Father's Day brunch atop the Seattle Space Needle. Trim light blue cardstock and adhere to orange cardstock. Cut strips of dark blue cardstock and attach with orange and blue eyelets. Crop and adhere photos. Print journaling on blue cardstock and adhere. Mat small cropped picture and accent with sheer ribbon, charm and words.

Joanna Bolick, Fletcher, North Carolina

Supplies: Blue and orange textured cardstocks (Bazzill); charm (www.twopeasinabucket.com); blue eyelets; orange eyelets; ribbon

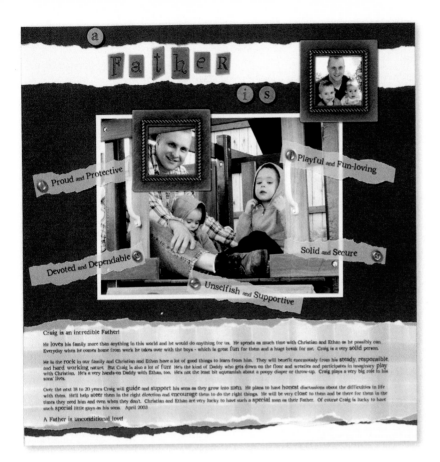

A Father Is

Patricia highlighted her husband's admirable characteristics by typing each on vellum and attaching them to her page with eyelets. Tear ends of dark blue cardstock and layer on white. Tear patterned paper and adhere along the bottom of page. Print journaling on vellum, tear edges and place over patterned paper. Mat photo on white and place in the center of the page. Print journaling captions on vellum, tear apart and attach with screw eyelets. Place one metal frame over main photo and another at top of page with cropped photo inside. Use metal letters for title.

Patricia Anderson, Selah, Washington

Supplies: Blue and white textured cardstocks (Bazzill); patterned paper (Ivy Cottage Creations); frames, letter charms and eyelets (Making Memories); vellum

Daddy

Brandy chose muted coordinating patterns and a simple design to pay tribute to her husband on a Father's Day page. Trim, crumple, sand and ink patterned paper. Wrap with fiber and charm and attach to patterned background paper with brads. Mat photo on patterned paper and accent with circle clip; adhere to page. Print journaling on vellum, accent with strip of patterned paper and adhere to page. Cut title from cardstock with a craft knife. Finish with date stamp.

Brandy Logan, Hendersonville, North Carolina

Supplies: Patterned papers (Chatterbox); circle clip (Making Memories); fibers (On the Surface); charm (Paper Parachute); brads; stamping ink; vellum; date stamp

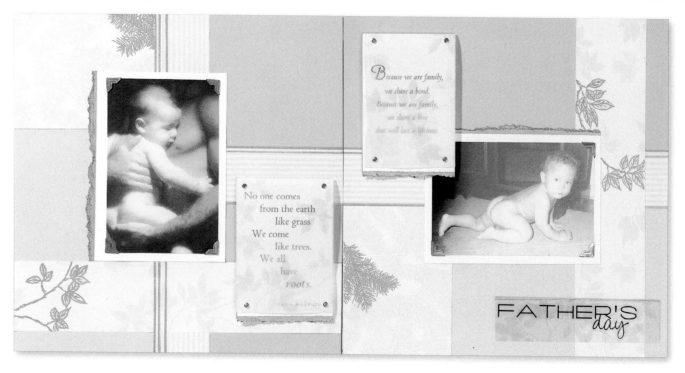

Father's Day

A fold-out element reveals details about Mary's son's heritage. Layer pieces of patterned paper over beige cardstock and trace around them with a gold paint pen. Mat photos with photo corners on white cardstock, tear along one side and color with gold. Fold white cardstock to create fold-out elements and attach journaling and photo to insides. Tear front edges and color with gold. Print journaling quotes on patterned paper; cover with vellum and attach to fold-outs with snaps. Add word stickers to strip of vellum for title and accent with gold pen.

Mary Walby, Royal Oak, Michigan

Supplies: Patterned papers and word stickers (EK Success); gold paint pen (Marvy); snaps (Doodlebug Design); photo corners; beige cardstock

Facts & Legends:

In the early 1900s, Senora Smart Dodd of Spokane, Washington, the originator of Father's Day, designated the rose as the holiday's symbol. If your father is living, you should wear a red rose on Father's Day. If your father has passed away, wear a white rose.

Try This:

Pay tribute to fathers both past and present in your family on a red and white spread. On a red background, place photos of modern-day fathers in your family, along with key words relevant to each person. On a white background, add photos and journaling of fathers who have passed away. Stamp subtle rose images for decoration.

Father's Day

Lindsay included a popular quote on her Father's Day page. Print quote on patterned paper, trim and layer on blue cardstock and place on patterned background paper. Mat photo with white, tan and blue cardstocks. Tear bottom edge of blue, wrap with fibers and accent with letter stickers and metal stars. Stamp date on page and accent with metal letters and embellishments.

Lindsay Teague, Phoenix, Arizona

Supplies: Patterned papers (Chatterbox); letter stickers, metal accents (Making Memories); date stamp (Office Max); stamping ink; blue, tan and white cardstocks; fibers

Dad 2002

Ruthann documented her children's excitement about giving their father his presents. Layer patterned paper on black cardstock. Mat photos on tan and gray cardstocks and adhere to page. Add quote sticker. Tear heart shape from red paper, adhere small strips of white and journal. Write on strip of vellum, allowing words to overlap onto heart. Cut "dad" from cardstock to match design on patterned paper and adhere to page with foam tape.

Ruthann Grabowski, Yorktown, Virginia

Supplies: Patterned paper (Autumn Leaves); quote sticker (Wordsworth); foam tape; black, gray, tan,white, blue and red cardstocks; vellum; black pen

THE
THI
ABO
g

Nomatter what day of the year,
it's always about the grandkids.
GRANDPARENTS DAY

SWEET
TREATS

PONY
RIDES

PAINTED
FACES

Labor Day Weekend ~ 1997

It's become somewhat of a tradition to spend
part of our Labor Day weekend at
Monmouth Park Racetrack. We get all the
cousins and family friends together for a fun
picnic, a few friendly wagers on the ponies
and a slew of fun activities for the kids.
There is so much to be done: what with all
the eating, drinking, face-painting, pony
rides, and cheering for our favorite horses,
it's really quite exhausting! No wonder they
call it Labor Day. We need a day off to
recover from our day off!

MIKAELA

LABOR
DAY

Picnic

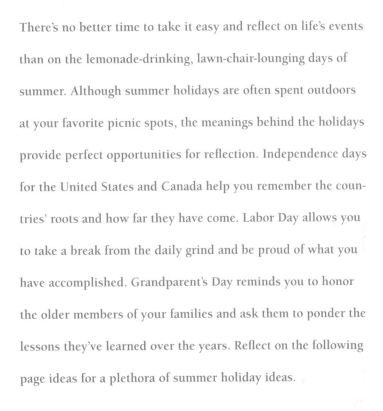

Summer *HOLIDAYS*

There's no better time to take it easy and reflect on life's events than on the lemonade-drinking, lawn-chair-lounging days of summer. Although summer holidays are often spent outdoors at your favorite picnic spots, the meanings behind the holidays provide perfect opportunities for reflection. Independence days for the United States and Canada help you remember the countries' roots and how far they have come. Labor Day allows you to take a break from the daily grind and be proud of what you have accomplished. Grandparent's Day reminds you to honor the older members of your families and ask them to ponder the lessons they've learned over the years. Reflect on the following page ideas for a plethora of summer holiday ideas.

Find Page Ideas For...

My First
Canada Day

Bela chose a childlike font to complement her son's first Canada Day. Print title on red cardstock, tear along bottom edge and mount on white cardstock. Mat photo on white and blue cardstocks, leaving room for button accents. Print journaling on vellum and attach to textured paper with square brads. Embellish metal-rimmed tag with letter stickers and date stamp.

Bela Luis, Winnipeg, Manitoba, Canada

Supplies: Textured paper (Provo Craft); tag and square brads (Making Memories); buttons (EK Success); letter stickers (Pioneer); red, white and blue cardstocks; vellum; string; embroidery floss

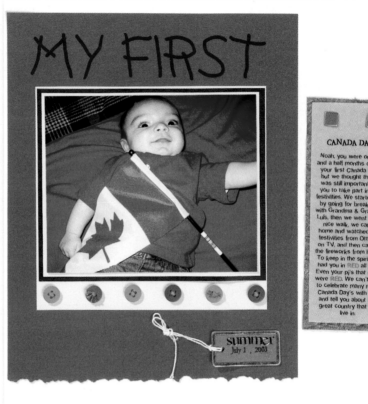

Oh Canada

Canada Day held special significance for the Macdonald family in 2003, as it was the year they took their Canadian citizenship tests. Create black edges on patterned papers by applying black pigment paint with a stipple brush. Tear, layer and roll edges of patterned paper for background; blacken rolled edges. Adhere photograph. Print Canadian anthem on patterned paper, blacken edges, mat with black cardstock and adhere over corner of photo with brads. Print other journaling on tan, cut apart, apply stamping ink to edges and adhere. Create title by using dimensional adhesive on letter stickers. Cut leaf shape from clay using a shape mold. When clay is dry, apply pigment paints and dimensional fluid to leaf. Add premade letters for title.

Colleen Macdonald, Calgary, Alberta, Canada

Supplies: Patterned papers (Karen Foster Design); black, gold and white pigment paints (AMACO); letter stickers (Creative Imaginations); brads and clay (Provo Craft); dimensional adhesive (Plaid); red pigment paint (Ranger); stamping ink; adhesive dots

Supplies: Die-cut letters and leaves (Create-a-Cut); flower eyelets (Stamp Doctor); red and white cardstock; foam tape

Canada Day 2002

Sharon's layout includes photos of neighbors, friends and relatives celebrating Canada Day. Crop photos and adhere along bottom of white background. Mat other photos on red cardstock. For title, layer die-cut letters on white and red and arrange through center of spread; accent with die-cut leaves and eyelets. Print journaling on white cardstock, mat and accent with leaf. Cut out portion of journaling in a separate square and adhere with foam tape.

Sharon Whitehead, Vernon, British Columbia, Canada

O Canada

Trudy's page captures anticipation before the Canada Day parade. Cut red patterned paper into maple leaf shape, cut in half and layer on white patterned paper. Create a 4" strip of red paper and adhere on left side. Accent page with cross-stitches. Sand and ink edges of photo, punch holes in corners and attach to page with safety pins. Place letter stickers on wood tiles and ink edges. Apply walnut ink to tags and stamp journaling. Accent with metal leaf, hemp and eyelets.

Trudy Sigurdson, Victoria, British Columbia, Canada
Photo: Shelley Sundher, Victoria, British Columbia, Canada

Supplies: Patterned papers (Karen Foster Design); letter stickers (Me & My Big Ideas); safety pins (Making Memories); letter stamps (PSX Design); metal leaf (Provo Craft); walnut ink (Fiber Scraps); date stamp; hemp cord; stamping inks; embroidery floss; eyelets; tags; wood tiles

Facts & Legends:

Canada Day observes the creation of the Canadian federal government on July 1, 1868. The British North America Act proclaimed that the provinces were "one dominion under the name of Canada." Thus, the holiday was known as Dominion Day until 1982. Today, it is celebrated much like the United States' 4th of July with parades, picnics and fireworks.

Try This:

Use "Dominion Day" or "One Dominion Under the Name of Canada" as a page title to pay tribute to the history of the holiday.

4th of July

Supplies (4th of July)

Supplies: Patterned paper, cardstocks, number stickers (Provo Craft); fibers (EK Success, On the Surface); lettering template (EK Success); eyelets (Making Memories); red and blue tissue papers; chalk

4th of July

Renee cut title letters from fireworks pictures to adorn her 4th of July page. Tear and layer patterned paper over red and blue tissue papers. Cut strips of red, white and blue cardstocks and adhere across spread. Mat photos and "hang" one photo using fibers and a brad. Cut title from duplicate photos using a lettering template, mount on white and red cardstocks; trim. Print journaling on a tag, tear edge and embellish with fibers.

Renee Villalobos-Campa, Winnebago, Illinois

Things I Really Love About the USA

Teri pays tribute to what she loves about celebrating Independence Day in her city. Tear light blue cardstock and layer on patterned paper, leaving open space across the top. Layer photo on patterned paper and dark gray cardstock; machine stitch around the edge and staple with premade star. Staple other premade embellishments to pieces of gray cardstock. Stamp words on white, trim into strips and arrange at top and bottom of page. Accent page with staples and write journaling with black pen.

Teri Anderson, Idaho Falls, Idaho

Supplies: Patterned paper and premade accents (EK Success); letter stamps (Hero Arts); stamping ink; light blue, gray and white cardstocks; black pen; thread; staples

80 Summer Holidays

Celebrate Freedom

Susan accented Independence Day photos with a title made of tiny red and white tags. Crop photos, mat on red and white cardstocks and adhere to page. Cut strips from panoramic flag photo and layer on photo mats. Place ribbon along the bottom of spread. Punch tag shapes and embellish with glitter glue, eyelets, fibers and chalk. Using a lettering template, cut title from the same panoramic flag photo and mount on tags. String fibers through tag eyelets and adhere to page. Write journaling on blue card-stock, layer on tag and embellish with photo strips and fibers.

Susan Kohlman, Maynard, Massachusetts

Supplies: White and red textured and blue speckled cardstocks (Bazzill); panoramic flag photo (Creative Imaginations); fibers (Fibers by the Yard); lettering template (Scrap Pagerz); tag punch (EK Success); blue vellum; ribbon; eyelets; metallic pen; glitter glue; chalk

Independence at Two

Brandi shows that "independence day" has a new meaning as her daughter starts to develop her own ideas. Layer embossed paper, red cardstock, definition paper and number paper on blue cardstock. Mat photo on white and red cardstocks and accent with metal corner accent and date stamp; adhere to page by applying adhesive to top and bottom edges. Print title on vellum and adhere to page with silver brads. Tear vellum, add rub-on word and attach over photo with brads. Write journaling on white cardstock, mat on black, add label and conceal behind photo mat.

Brandi Barnes, Kelso, Tennessee

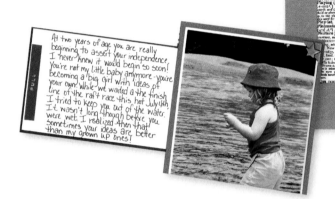

Supplies: Patterned papers (7 Gypsies); embossed paper (Provo Craft); blue textured cardstock (Bazzill); label maker (Dymo); date stamp, metal photo corner, brads and rub-on word (Making Memories); red cardstock; vellum; stamping ink

Remembering the Past

Joanna's journaling teaches her son about the freedoms he is blessed with in the United States. Tear red cardstock and layer on script patterned paper. Print journaling on light blue cardstock and trim to allow room for photo. Mat on dark blue cardstock and attach strip of star patterned paper over photo. Tear brown cardstock and layer on white. Print title, allowing words to cover both papers, cut apart, ink edges and accent with silver snaps. Embellish design with star sticker and fibers strung through eyelets.

Joanna Bolick, Fletcher, North Carolina

Supplies: Script patterned paper (Karen Foster Design); star patterned paper (Sandylion); star sticker (EK Success); blue, red, white and tan cardstock; snaps; eyelets; stamping ink; fibers

Celebrating the 4th

Aubrey included a quote about freedom as her journaling. Trim edges of red cardstock and layer on blue for background. Round corners of photos with star corner punch; mat on cream and blue cardstocks and attach to page. Cut strips of red cardstock, layer on cream and add blue paper with star eyelets to create flag. Mat cream on blue for other areas of page; accent blocks with stitching, metal letters, star brads, punched shapes, buttons and chalk. Write title and journaling on two blocks.

Aubrey Pena, Tucson, Arizona

Supplies: Blue, red and cream textured cardstocks (Bazzill); metal letters and star eyelets (Making Memories); star corner punch (Carl); heart and star punches (EK Success); brads; buttons; black pen

Facts & Legends:

The colors of the American flag were not given specific meaning at the time the flag was designed. Later in 1782, Charles Thomson, Secretary of the Continental Congress, reported on the symbolism of red, white and blue as they appeared on the Great Seal of the United States: "White signifies purity and innocence; red, hardiness and valor; and blue...signifies vigilance, perseverance and justice."

Try This:

Search the Internet for pictures of the Great Seal of the United States and its meaning. For a new twist on your next 4th of July page, include a picture of the Seal and the information you discover, along with the significance of red, white and blue.

Dreams Can Go Wild

Kelli used lyrics from one of her daughter's favorite songs as the journaling on her page. Tear patterned paper and layer on brown cardstock. Mat photo on blue cardstock, layer on patterned paper and ink the torn edges. Layer torn patterned paper, brads, nailheads, mesh and string on tags. Crumble and ink premade letters and add to tags along with letter stickers to create title.

Kelli Lawlor, Norfolk, Virginia

Supplies: Patterned papers (Provo Craft); premade letters (Foofala); letter stickers (EK Success); wax linen (7 Gypsies); stamping ink and nailheads (Club Scrap); brown cardstock; brads; chalk; black pen

All American Girl

Holly chose a muted color scheme, allowing photos of her daughter to stand out. Tear script paper and layer on flag patterned paper. Adhere photos to background. Print journaling and cut out letters on cream paper; stain letters and journaling block with a moist tea bag. Color metal stars and frame with copper paint. Place metal frame over cropped picture and accent page with metal stars. Place letter stickers on tags, tie with hemp and weave through title letters on page.

Holly VanDyne, Mansfield, Ohio

Supplies: Script patterned paper (7 Gypsies); flag patterned paper (source unknown); metal frame, star snaps and metal star (Making Memories); letter stickers (Wordsworth); lettering template (C-Thru Ruler); metallic paint (Renkly); hemp; tea bag

American Baby

Supplies: Cardstock (Bazzill); patterned paper and accent stickers (Karen Foster Design); star stickers (EK Success); chalk (Close To My Heart); star brads (Creative Impressions); metal circles (Making Memories); hemp

Patty used expressive pictures conveying the sense of freedom. Cut patterned papers and arrange at angles behind photos; accent with star brads and stickers. Mat enlarged photo on patterned paper, roll back the edges and chalk. Print title on patterned paper and accent with hemp and star sticker.

Patty Browne, Boone, North Carolina

American Kids

Christy created patterned paper by printing phrases describing America on vellum. Layer two shades of blue patterned paper on red cardstock; then layer with printed vellum. Mat photo on blue cardstock; tear bottom edge and embellish with fibers, stamped tag, punched metal daisy and button. Cut pieces of red and blue papers and layer with letter stickers. Add fibers to one paper square. Accent page with red buttons.

Christy Tomlinson for Chatterbox, Inc., Nampa, Idaho

Supplies: Patterned papers (Chatterbox, Karen Foster Design); letter stickers (SEI); fibers (Rustic Treasures); buttons (Junkitz); number stamps (Hero Arts); metal tag (Making Memories); vellum; eyelets; foil sheet; daisy punch

Supplies: Patterned paper (Karen Foster Design); brads, snaps, tags and metal letters (Making Memories); twill tape and walnut ink (7 Gypsies); conchos (Scrapworks); fibers (EK Success); letter template (C-Thru Ruler); blue cardstock; chalk; jump rings; fishing swivels

America

Julie created a fold-out design teaching her son the importance of respecting others in a free country. Tape two pieces of blue cardstock together. Create a score line 6" in from each side to create outer flaps. Attach another piece of blue cardstock between score lines. Layer patterned paper over blue and on inside of flaps. Mat photos on blue cardstock. Tear the bottom of two photo mats and accent with fibers. Embellish one photo mat with tags hanging from metal fishing swivels. Place metal letters on tags. Adhere twill tape border and embellish with conchos. Create flag by tearing red and cream cardstocks into strips; place on blue and accent with star mesh snaps. For fronts of flaps, adhere patterned paper, tear edges and add title cut from lettering templates. Apply walnut ink to title and accent with silver brads.

Julie Johnson, Seabrook, Texas

4th of July

Strips of coordinating patterned paper create a clean backdrop for Mary's black-and-white photos. Trim patterned papers and adhere to white backgrounds. Cut strips of patterned paper and attach to white cardstock and patterned paper with eyelets and snaps. Weave colored raffia through eyelets. Mat photos on white and blue cardstocks with white photo corners. Attach one photo to folded white cardstock; adhere journaling inside fold-out. For other photo, print words on vellum, tear edge and slip into photo corners in front of photo. Tear piece of vellum and add letter sticker for title; mat vellum and add eyelets and raffia.

Mary Walby, Royal Oak, Michigan
Photo: Stacey Totzke, Oak Park, Michigan

Supplies: Patterned papers (Hot Off The Press); letter stickers (EK Success); eyelets and snaps (Making Memories); photo corners (Canson); raffia; white and blue cardstocks; vellum

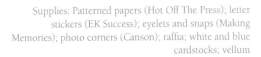

Our Little Patriot

Andrea created an eclectic design rich with fabric accents and sewing notions. Trim blue cardstock and layer over red; stitch edges. Weave red and blue embroidery floss through mesh and adhere to page. Stitch fabric strip over mesh, add metal letters, star snaps and safety pins. Print title on tan, tear out, chalk edges and machine stitch to fabric strip. Print journaling, machine stitch to fabric and paper; accent with safety pins and charm. Punch holes in one side of photo and weave embroidery floss through; finish with ribbon charms. Mat photos on white cardstock and adhere to page. Add premade flag and star die cuts. Place slide mount over printed date. Hand stitch around page elements with embroidery floss. Finish page with buttons.

Andrea Lyn Vetten-Marley, Aurora, Colorado

Supplies: Metal letters, star eyelets and ribbon charms (Making Memories); premade flag and stars (EK Success); slide mount (Designer's Library); charm (Watch Us); mesh (Magic Mesh); red, white, blue and tan cardstocks; fabric; buttons; safety pins; embroidery floss; chalk

4th of July 2003

Misty placed photos of sparklers inside slide mounts for emphasis. Place patterned paper on white cardstock. Mat photos on red cardstock and adhere to page. Place rickrack border along the bottom of the page. Create flag by layering torn pieces of cardstock; accent with red tags. Tear stars and adhere to top of page. Print journaling on vellum and embellish with buttons; layer over background stars. Adhere glitter to slide mounts using double-sided tape and embellish with beads and star buttons. Crop photos to fit slide mounts and adhere over rickrack.

Misty Posey, Decatur, Alabama

Supplies: Patterned paper (Kopp Design); glitter (Magic Scraps); star buttons (Jesse James); slide mounts (Jest Charming); fibers (Fibers by the Yard); tag die cuts (QuicKutz); white, red and blue cardstocks; beads; eyelets; rickrack

Noah's Independence Day

Jennifer journaled about how her son declared his independence when he started saying "Mom" instead of "Mommy." Cut pieces of blue, red and white cardstocks and layer on white background. Print journaling on brown cardstock and adhere to page. Punch stars from red, white, and blue and position next to journaling. Mat photo on blue cardstock and adhere. Create title with die-cut letters. Punch stars from sheet metal and adhere to white strip. Cut star shape from tag; back with red paper covered in double-sided tape. Apply tiny glass marbles to star cut-out and ink the front of tag.

Jennifer Lessinger, Rockville, Minnesota

Supplies: Star punch (EK Success); letter die cuts (source unknown); tag (Making Memories); white, blue, red, brown cardstocks; glass marbles; stamping ink; metal sheet; double-sided tape

4th of July

Chris listed some of her daughter's favorite 4th of July traditions. Layer patterned transparency over flag patterned paper. Tear each side of brown patterned paper and place on top of transparency. Trim red paper, lightly sand the edges and attach with star brads. Adhere photo on red paper. Print journaling on a transparency; trim and adhere to red paper. Use tag and letter stickers for title. Cut tag using template and layer with film, metal star and Scrabble letter. Cut piece of metal screen and staple over items to form pocket on the tag. Attach safety pin, tag sticker and date on top of screen pocket. Accent tag with a circle clip. Lightly sand the edges of preprinted flag die cut and adhere to page. Staple screen over bottom of flag.

Chris Douglas, East Rochester, Ohio

Supplies: Patterned papers (Creative Imaginations, Karen Foster Design, Pebbles); patterned transparency (K & Company); jump rings, circle clip, star charm, tile letter sticker (Making Memories); flag die cut (Cropper Hopper); tag template (Deluxe Designs); tag sticker (Pebbles); letter stickers (Provo Craft); safety pin; staples; screen; brad; camera film

Born in the USA

Heather's young daughter was content to simply play with a flag on her first 4th of July, which her photo highlights. Trim star patterned paper and layer over stripes paper; machine stitch strips of fabric and patterned paper to background. Mat photo on white cardstock and adhere with foam tape. Color tag with walnut ink and embellish with ribbon, metal letters and hanging tag. Stamp words and adhere to background and metal tag.

Heather Melzer, Yorkville, Illinois

Supplies: Patterned papers (Karen Foster Design, Wübie); tag (Avery); letter stamps (Hero Arts, PSX Design); metal letters and tag (Rustic Treasures); date stamp (Making Memories); white cardstock; ribbon; brad; stamping ink; fabric

Labor Day

No Labor Today

Cori chose a single enlarged photo to represent her family's labor day excursion. Place enlarged photo on light blue cardstock. Cut thin strips of dark and light blue cardstocks; adhere at top and bottom of page. On white cardstock rectangle, add die cut, vellum, pebble letters, metal label holder and fibers.

Cori Dahmen, Portland, Oregon

Supplies: Light and dark blue cardstocks; die cut, book plates, pebble letters (Li'l Davis Designs); chalk (Stampin' Up!); fibers (Fiber Scraps)

The Labor Day Parade

Jennifer's page pays tribute to small-town parades. Trim green patterned paper and place on blue background. Adhere strips of green and tan cardstocks near top. Cut a 5" wide piece of black cardstock. With a craft knife, cut square from black and adhere mesh behind. Mat photo on white and place on black. Layer strips of white and black and attach to page with eyelets across bottom. Hang photo from mesh using star eyelets, metal chain and checkered ribbon. Trim photo and journaling to fit on tags; accent with ribbon, safety pins, rivets, star and heart bead. Use letter beads, wire and pebble letters for title.

Jennifer Gallacher, Savannah, Georgia

Supplies: Patterned paper (Colors by Design); pebble letters, chain, metal label holder and safety pins (Li'l Davis Designs); mesh (Gotta Mesh); ribbon (Offray); star punch (EK Success); snaps, wire and brads (Making Memories); blue, white, black, brown and red cardstocks

Facts & Legends:

Since 1969, a Fairfax, Virginia, church has celebrated Labor Day by holding a "Blessing of the Tools" event to recognize the labor of its members. All attendees bring a tool of their trade to be blessed, whether it's a meat thermometer or a pocket calculator. Afterward, they have a picnic, which members claim the 133-year-old church has held "before there was even a Labor Day."

Try This:

This Labor Day, in addition to the traditional family picnic spread you might make, pay tribute to yourself and your "labor" of love—scrapbooking. Have a family member take a picture of you holding a favorite page, in addition to close-up shots of your favorite tools of the trade—from crop caddies to craft knives. Journal about why scrapbooking is a labor of love for you.

Labor Day

Bright patterns create energy on Jennifer's Labor Day page. Layer peach, white and green paper strips across top of blue patterned background. Mat photo with white, orange and patterned papers; adhere to page. Stamp names on slide mount and small premade frames; decorate with ribbon, flower stamp, buttons, eyelets and string. Crop photos to fit inside each. Print title on a transparency and machine stitch to patterned paper cut into tag shape. Accent title with concho letters, square tag, cut-outs, rivet and ribbon.

Jennifer Gallacher, Savannah, Georgia

Supplies: Green patterned paper, premade frames, flower cut-out (KI Memories); blue patterned paper (Paper Fever); peach patterned papers, cardstock, tag and eyelets (Making Memories); flower stamp (Imaginations); slide mount (Magic Scraps); ribbon (Offray); letter stamps (PSX Design); conchos and letters (Scrapworks); white rivet (Chatterbox); stamping ink; transparency; thread

Lazy Labor Day Picnic

A woven handmade paper picnic basket serves as the focal point of Samantha's Labor Day page. Layer tan and patterned paper on rust cardstock. Print journaling on patterned paper, tear sides and adhere to page. Layer paper strips across top of page. Punch squares and add letter stickers to each for title. Trim edges of squares with decorative scissors. Silhouette cut subjects and grass from photos and cover the bottom ⅔" of the page. To make basket, cut ⅛" strips of brown cardstock and ½" strips of tan; weave together. Form basket handles by attaching two paper strips with an eyelet to top center of basket; bend ends of strips behind basket. Attach more eyelets across top of basket. Place fabric behind basket and attach to page.

Samantha Walker, Battle Ground, Washington

Supplies: Patterned papers and letter stickers (Chatterbox); fabric (Carole Fabrics); eyelets; green, tan, brown and rust cardstocks; decorative scissors; square punch

Grandparents

A single casual photo and simple sentiment honors grandparents on Jennifer's page. Cut strips of light blue cardstock in various widths and adhere to dark blue cardstock. Print title and journaling on light blue cardstock, trim into wide strip and accent with fern leaves. Mat photo on light blue cardstock and patterned paper. Place sheer green ribbon above and below picture and embellish with green buttons.

Jennifer Lamb, Rolesville, North Carolina

Supplies: Patterned paper (C-Thru Ruler); button, ribbon (Making Memories); botanical fern stickers (Darice); light and dark blue cardstocks

Two Grandparents, Five Grandchildren

Pam documented the first Grandparent's Day in which all the kids were with their grandparents at the same time. Adhere photos on patterned paper background and attach rickrack in between. Print journaling, trim and ink edges and adhere to page with fibers and rivets. For title, stamp letters in two colors on strip of paper, ink edges and brush with white acrylic paint. Color slide mounts with acrylic paint and use to frame portions of the title.

Pam Canavan, Clermont, Florida

Supplies: Patterned paper and rivets (Chatterbox); fibers (Fibers by the Yard); rickrack (ScrapTherapy Designs); letter stamps (PSX Design); acrylic paint (Delta); slide mounts (Loersch); stamping inks

Day of the Grandparent

Torrey relates her grandmother's character traits to the year she was born, as based on the Chinese calendar. Her embellishments carry out the theme. Rub brown ink into the edges of green cardstock and layer on black cardstock. Repeat technique for terra cotta papers and layer. Stamp Chinese symbols on terra cotta paper. Accent with brads at the corners of all cardstocks. Attach mesh ribbon to one side with brads. Print journaling and Chinese symbols on vellum and heat set with embossing powder; tear edges and rub with ink. Attach to wooden sticks and adhere to page; add jewelry elements to sticks near bottom. Mat photo on white cardstock, mesh and terra cotta cardstock. Embellish with brads and adhere to page with foam tape. Create title with letter stickers.

Torrey Miller, Thornton, Colorado

Supplies: Mesh paper (Magenta); Chinese stamp (All Night Media); letter stickers (Creative Imaginations); wooden sticks (Darice); black, green and terra cotta cardstocks; embossing powder; mesh ribbon; stamping inks; jewelry elements; brads

Together

Trudy's journaling talks about how lucky her children are to live close to their grandparents. Ink the edges of all papers and photo with a brown inkpad. Brush white acrylic paint along one side of patterned paper and print journaling on top. Add buttons, twill tape dipped in walnut ink, safety pin, washer and charm around journaling. Adhere patterned paper to background and layer photo over it. Paint metal title letters with white paint and attach with dimensional adhesive. Place metal photo holders near the corners of photo.

Trudy Sigurdson, Victoria, British Columbia, Canada

Supplies: Patterned papers (Chatterbox); metal letters, photo holders, washer and safety pins (Making Memories); brads (ScrapArts); charm (Blue Moon Beads); acrylic paint (Plaid); walnut ink (Fiber Scraps); stamping ink; twill tape; buttons

Facts & Legends:

The holiday honoring the oldest members of our families is historically one of the United States' most recent observances. West Virginia native Marian McQuade, a mother of 15 and grandmother of 40, first began to lobby for Grandparent's Day to help combat the loneliness that many elderly people experience while living in nursing homes. President Jimmy Carter signed the resolution to make it an official holiday in 1978.

Try This:

Gather bits of trivia about Grandma or Grandpa and weave the information onto a Grandparents Day page. Ask them questions such as "What was your first job like?" "How much did your first car cost?" and "When did you start dating?"

Autumn HOLIDAYS

The landscapes become more colorful in autumn as leaves turn shades of red, orange, gold and brown. But just as vibrant are the holidays you celebrate at this time of year. On October 31, costumes worn by children as they scurry from door to door pepper the neighborhoods with color. Thanksgiving dinner tables are set with shining flatware, crystal glasses, table cloths and centerpieces in festive shades. Even more colorful and rich in tradition are the three Jewish holidays in autumn and the history they represent. Browse the following ideas to inspire pages that are colorful and interesting in all respects.

Supplies: Metallic and patterned papers (Sandylion); title die cuts (Griff's Shortcuts); star die cuts (Ellison); charms (source unknown); eyelets; vellum; black pen

Rosh Hashanah

Through a variety of photos, Marni captured the joy of celebrating the Jewish New Year. Mat pictures on metallic paper; adhere other photos directly to patterned background. Write journaling on vellum and frame with star die cut; add another die cut to opposite side. Mount die-cut titles on vellum and adhere to page with silver eyelets. Accent with metal charms.

Marni Kaner, Dallas, Texas

May You Have a Sweet Year

Laurie displayed symbols of hope in the Jewish tradition of Rosh Hashanah. Layer patterned paper on green cardstock. Mat photos on green cardstock. Shade yellow paper with ink and a stipple brush; mat on green and apply letter stickers. Write journaling on patterned paper and add flower pebbles. Accent page with bee die cuts.

Laurie Gore, Bonita, California

Supplies: Patterned paper (NRN Designs); bee die cuts (Deluxe Designs); letters stickers (Creative Imaginations); flower pebbles (Pressed Petals); green and yellow cardstocks; stamping ink; black pen

Sukkot / Yom Kippur

Sukkot

Marni adapted premade embellishments to create symbols that represent Sukkot. Mat photos on olive cardstock and adhere to textured paper. Stamp gold paper with leaf images and letter stamps; use to mat one photo and cut into tags. Crop photos and add to tags. Print journaling on cardstock, cut apart and adhere to page. Write journaling on terra cotta paper and accent with burlap. Combine premade fruit and leaf embellishments to accent journaling. Color premade wheat embellishment with green ink; combine with paper strips and wrap with wire and raffia to create holiday symbolic branch.

Marni Kaner, Dallas, Texas

Supplies: letter stamps (Hero Arts); leaf stamps (Close To My Heart, Stampin' Up!); tag template (Provo Craft); premade embellishments (EK Success); burlap; handmade paper; terra cotta, gold and olive cardstocks; raffia; black pen

Yom Kippur

Carrying on a family tradition, Debbie took her son shopping for special clothes to wear on Yom Kippur. Stamp title on brown cardstock, trim and layer on black cardstock; accent with metal letters. Trim cream paper, ink the edges and adhere over brown. Create mini album by matting pictures on black cardstock, punching holes in the sides of each and securing with metal chains and charm. Print journaling and adhere to tan cardstock. Attach transparency envelope over journaling to form a pocket and accent the front with beads. Slip mini album inside pocket. Embellish design with metal label holder and square concho.

Debbie De Mars, Overland Park, Kansas

Supplies: Metal letters, brads, chain (Making Memories); letter stamps (Hero Arts, Ma Vinci's); concho (Scrapworks); transparency envelope (Creative Memories); beads (Blue Moon Beads); metal label holder (Magic Scraps); black, brown and cream cardstocks; stamping ink; foam tape; charm

Supplies: Patterned paper (Design Originals); metal frames (Making Memories); blue and cream cardstocks; embroidery floss; fibers; buttons; snaps; mesh; chalk; eyelets; thread

The Perfect Pumpkin

Andrea used a variety of stitches to embellish a Halloween page. Cut irregular shapes from corners of light blue cardstock and mount on dark blue cardstock. Layer with mesh at the top and bottom. Mat photos on cream cardstock, adhere to page and hand stitch around edges. Print title and journaling on cream cardstock; tear and chalk the edges. Machine stitch journaling strips and title throughout the design. Tear and chalk pieces of patterned paper and machine stitch to layout. Accent with buttons and snaps. Wrap metal frames with fiber and adhere to page.

Andrea Lyn Vetten-Marley, Aurora, Colorado

Dressed to Go

Janice's journaling describes how her son changed his mind about his costume at the last possible minute. Cut a strip of brown cardstock, weave it through a metal ribbon charm and adhere to cream background. Cut 6" piece of green cardstock and place on page. Print title and journaling on orange and cream cardstocks, trim and place on green. Mat photo on orange and brown cardstocks. Stamp names on premade circles. Stamp date on orange cardstock and adhere to page.

Janice Carson, Hamilton, Ontario, Canada

Supplies: Cream, orange, brown and green textured cardstocks (Bazzill); premade circles (KI Memories); ribbon charm (Making Memories); letter stamps (Hero Arts)

Abbey's Pumpkin

At first, Amanda's dog wasn't impressed with her pumpkin—until she took a taste. Mat both photos on one piece of cream cardstock; adhere to brown background. Punch circles from cardstock and patterned paper and apply to metal-rimmed tags. Embellish design with circle tags. Print title on cream cardstock, trim, crumple and attach with copper brads. Journal with a black pen on background.

Amanda Goodwin, Munroe Falls, Ohio

Supplies: Patterned paper (Karen Foster Design); brown and cream cardstocks; brads; black pen

Our House on Halloween

Supplies: Tag (Making Memories); bat (Frances Meyer); white cardstock

As a child Heather loved to trick-or-treat, so she decorates her house specially for the neighborhood kids. Print title and journaling on white cardstock. Accent title with a black metal-rimmed tag and bat cut from patterned paper. Use image-editing software to print "Our" in white over a photo for part of title. Crop photos and adhere directly to background, overlapping in some areas.

Heather Melzer, Yorkville, Illinois

Halloween House

In her neighborhood, Jeniece's home is well-known for its Halloween decorations, including a fog machine and bubble maker. Cut strips of brown corduroy fabric and affix with staples around page border. Wipe the edges of pictures with copper ink and adhere to textured background. Create title letters and mount on background and over skeleton leaf using various media, including letter stamps, ink, fabric, leather, mica, burlap, metal, wood, string, safety pins and buttons. Print journaling on vellum, wipe with stamping ink and attach over photo with staples. Accent page with washer.

Jeniece Higgins, Lake Forest, Illinois

Supplies: Textured paper and metal letter tag (Provo Craft); small metal letters, safety pins (Making Memories); letter stamps and stencil (Ma Vinci's); fibers (Fibers by the Yard); nameplate (Nunn Design); mica (USArtQuest); leather tag (Rusty Pickle); stamping ink; vellum; dried flowers; burlap; washer; canvas; bamboo clips; domino; Scrabble letter; button; corduroy fabric; copper leafing pen; skeleton leaf

Childhood Memories of Halloween

Pam created a heritage layout of her childhood memories at Halloween. Cut strips of orange paper and adhere to black cardstock at top and bottom of page. Tear the edge of two patterned papers. Layer and adhere to page. Apply crackle medium paint to premade frame, offset picture within frame. Emboss die-cut label holder with copper powder, stamp date on paper and place inside holder; adhere to frame. Alter a premade hanging tag with mesh, brad, sticker and die cut letters; hang from frame. Place letter stickers across bottom. Print journaling on a transparency and attach to page. Cut tags using template; embellish with eyelets and fiber. Place photos on tags and house in vellum envelope.

Pam Sivage, Georgetown, Texas

Supplies: Patterned papers (Provo Craft); label holder die cut and letters (QuickKutz); mesh (Magic Mesh); star eyelets (Making Memories); poem stone sticker (Creative Imaginations); tag template (Deluxe Designs); premade frame (My Mind's Eye); fence die cut (Sizzix); date stamp (PSX Design); premade hanging tag (EK Success); vellum envelope (source unknown); brown, black and orange cardstocks; transparency; wire; brad; fibers

Halloween 1998

Robin included journaling in a decorative pocket that describes her thoughts at the time she took this photo of her son. Cut a 6" piece of patterned paper and layer on brown cardstock. Brush white acrylic paint on torn cardboard and place on page. Use image-editing software to alter color of picture before printing. Lightly sand edges of picture and mat on white cardstock. Ink the edges of cardstock with brown stamping ink. Print journaling on vellum, tear edges, crumple and attach over photo with acrylic nail. Ink edges of library pocket and embellish with torn paper, mesh, vintage card image, labels, plastic tie, moon charm and compass. Print journaling, fold, stamp words on one side and slip into pocket.

Robin Hohenstern, Brooklyn Park, Minnesota

Supplies: Brown textured cardstock (Bazzill); patterned papers (Karen Foster Design, Rusty Pickle); label maker (Dymo); moon charm (American Traditional); mesh (Magenta); acrylic nail (Chatterbox); letter stamps (Hero Arts); vintage card image; white cardstock; stamping ink; library pocket; cardboard; acrylic paint; vellum; plastic tie; compass

Supplies: Patterned papers (Chatterbox); label maker (Dymo); "Halloween" letter sticker (Pebbles); "costume" letter stickers (Wordsworth); "boy" letter stamps (Stampin' Up!); "October," spider and web stickers (EK Success); brown and black cardstocks; stamping ink; embossing powder; black pen

A Typical Boy Halloween Costume

Libby's son insisted on being the Grim Reaper for Halloween, and comments from others about it being a "boy" costume inspired her title. Ink the edges of brown cardstock, trim patterned paper, ink edges and adhere to brown. Sand the edges of pictures and mat on black cardstock. Adhere pictures to page, overlapping slightly. Combine patterned paper, various stickers, stamps and label tape to create title and date. Embellish page with 3-D spider stickers and journal with a black pen.

Libby Weifenbach, Bentonville, Arkansas

Facts & Legends:

Many practices associated with the holiday Americans know as Halloween stem from ancient Celtic beliefs. The Celts celebrated a festival called Samhain (pronounced sah-ween) on October 31, the eve of their new year. On this night, they believed spirits of the dead returned to mingle with the living. They celebrated by lighting bonfires, offering animal and crop sacrifices and dressing up in costumes. In the eighth century, a pope declared November 1 to be All Saint's Day as a way to give Christian symbolism to the ancient Celtic practices. This day was also known as All Hallow's Day, making October 31 All Hallow's Eve, which became known as Halloween.

Try This:

Use "All Hallow's Eve" as a page title instead of the traditional "Halloween."

Indiana Sam

After watching Indiana Jones, Cynthia's son transformed himself into Indiana Sam. Fold map patterned paper; sand and ink each crease. Adhere to brown cardstock. Mat photos on brown cardstocks and ink the edges; adhere photos to page. Print journaling on patterned paper and ink the edges. Layer journaling blocks over postcard patterned paper and accent with metal clips. Print title on elastic strip and attach with brads. Attach another elastic strip across top left corner.

Cynthia Coulon, Provo, Utah

Supplies: Patterned papers (Karen Foster Design, Rusty Pickle); metal clips (Pebbles); elastic (www.scrapfindings.com); light and dark brown cardstocks; stamping ink; brads

The Halloween Not So Great Photo Shoot

Joanna learned it's easier to take a mobile toddler to a professional photographer than to do it herself. Cut a 7" inch piece of plum cardstock and layer it on a brown background. Cut orange cardstock 4" wide and layer partially over plum. Adhere photo to left side. Print single words on brown and orange paper, trim into strips and apply at the top and bottom of page; embellish with buttons. Frame smaller photos with slide mounts and adhere to page; accent with premade clay word. Layer letter stickers and premade clay word over orange for title. Print journaling, mat on gold cardstock and adhere to page, slightly overlapping photo.

Joanna Bolick, Fletcher, North Carolina
Photo: The Picture People, Asheville, North Carolina

Supplies: Brown and gold textured cardstocks (Bazzill); letter stickers (Me & My Big Ideas, Wordsworth); buttons (SEI); clay words (EK Success); slide mounts (Designer's Library); plum and orange cardstocks

Bewitchingly Beautiful

Robin's 10-month-old daughter was distracted by the leaves in her photo shoot, resulting in this photo. Trim and layer brown cardstock and patterned papers, completely covering background. Cut a strip of black cardstock, machine stitch two rows and adhere across top of page. Mat picture with photo corners on patterned paper. Accent with ruler sticker. Embellish tag accent with heritage image, skeleton leaf, fiber, title and caption. Create title using various embellishments and letter stickers. Stamp name on patterned paper and frame with metal label holder.

Robin Hohenstern, Brooklyn Park, Minnesota

Supplies: Patterned papers (Colorbök, Creative Imaginations, DieCuts with a View, Hot Off The Press); photo corners; metal label holder (www.twopeasinabucket.com); fibers, ruler sticker (EK Success); "boo" cut-out (Foofala); letter stickers (Colorbök, Creative Imaginations, EK Success, Making Memories, Me & My Big Ideas); embellished letters (Foofala, Making Memories, Sweetwater); ribbon tag (Hirschberg, Schutz & Co.); letter stamps (Hero Arts); black, brown and pumpkin cardstock; skeleton leaf; eyelets; brads; stamping ink; foam tape; thread

The Costume that I Made

Jamie chose a clean, simple layout to showcase the Halloween costume she made. Print title and journaling on peach cardstock. Mat photo on a darker shade of peach and adhere to background. Print caption on cardstock and trim to fit inside slide mount. Adhere slide mount at top left-hand corner of photo.

Jamie Anderson, Lakemoor, Illinois

Supplies: Peach textured cardstocks (Bazzill); slide mount

Supplies: Patterned paper (Paper Adventures); tags (Making Memories); Halloween stickers (EK Success); fibers (Fibers by the Yard); blue cardstock; vellum

Making Madeline a Witch

Susan documented the process of getting her daughter's Halloween costume ready. Cut 4" strips of patterned paper and layer on blue cardstock. Print title and journaling on vellum, cut apart and adhere to page. Mat photos on black cardstock and across spread. Accent with metal-rimmed tags embellished with Halloween stickers.

Susan Bascom, Birmingham, Alabama

One Elmo Halloween

Susan designed a page equation-style to cleverly list the components of her son's Halloween. Print title and journaling on white cardstock. Trim and layer on orange patterned paper. Adhere photos, overlapping slightly. Create name and date with label maker and attach to page.

Susan Cyrus, Broken Arrow, Oklahoma

Supplies: Patterned paper (Bo-Bunny Press); label maker (Dymo); white cardstock

I Want My Mummy

Nancy's son's mummy costume was held together with safety pins, a concept that Nancy applied to her page design. Apply spray adhesive to cream cardstock and wrap with cheesecloth. Add tint to cheesecloth by spritzing with tea from a spray bottle. Mat photo on black cardstock. Tear center from patterned paper and use to frame photo; roll edges of patterned paper. Embellish frame with metal chain and torn pieces of corrugated and patterned papers. Print title letters, tear edges and mat on brown and black cardstocks; accent with safety pins. Stamp words on punched circle with brown ink. Print journaling on cardstock and mat with brown and black cardstocks; accent with corrugated paper and safety pins. Clip additional safety pins on background.

Nancy Freebairn, Layton, Utah

Supplies: Brown patterned paper (EK Success); patterned paper (Scrap Ease); metal chain (Darice); letter stamps (PSX Design); cheesecloth; safety pins; black and cream cardstocks; eyelet; corrugated paper

Decisions, Decisions

Cheryl records her son's "big decision" about choosing candy from his Halloween bounty before going to bed. Trim patterned papers and cardstock, ink edges and attach to orange background with black photo corners. Adhere photo to page with black photo corners. Print title on brown cardstock, trim and attach to burlap with safety pins. Create date accent with label maker.

Cheryl Overton, Kelowna, British Columbia, Canada

Supplies: Patterned papers (Daisy D's); light and dark orange cardstocks; safety pins; photo corners; label tape; stamping ink

Pumpkin Princess

Dana's daughter, dressed as a fairy princess, inspired her title. Print title on patterned paper and layer with torn strips of patterned paper. Mat photo with torn cream cardstock and accent edges with metallic rub-ons. Tear patterned papers and layer over cream cardstock; print journaling over layers and trim into tag shapes. Embellish tags with gold string and pumpkin charm. Accent page with pumpkin sticker and thread gold string through layout at various points.

Dana Swords, Fredericksburg, Virginia

Supplies: Patterned papers and pumpkin sticker (Karen Foster Design); pumpkin charm (All The Extras); string; metallic rub-ons; brown and cream cardstocks

Supplies: 3-D pumpkin and sign stickers (Westrim); letter stamps (PSX Design); orange acrylic paint (Delta); modeling paste (Liquitex); light orange and white cardstocks; burlap; stamping ink; candy wrappers; paper bag

Trick or Treat Sweets

A thick layer of modeling paste and paint creates a unique backdrop for Jeniece's photos. Cut ⅓" from left side of one piece of watercolor paper. Cover white cardstock with modeling paste to create texture. Paint over paste with orange acrylic paint. Print words on light orange cardstock and adhere to back of painted cut piece. Adhere burlap squares and pumpkin stickers to orange cardstock; brush edges with paint. Attach burlap square and strip to background pages. Print journaling, trim and adhere to burlap square. Stamp words on small paper bag and sign embellishment. Attach sign to bag, insert candy wrappers and adhere to burlap strip. Adhere one photo directly to burlap strip; mat others on orange cardstock and tear edges. Punch holes in corners of one mat and thread burlap strands through.

Jeniece Higgins, Lake Forest, Illinois

Halloween Memories

Denise compared her son's tastes in costumes at two different stages of his life. Tear patterned papers, layer on cardstock and roll back torn edges. Embellish photo frames with mesh, buttons, raffia, charms, and beads. Stamp title on each frame and heat set with orange embossing powder. Silhouette pumpkin photo and adhere with foam tape. Create envelope out of colored vellum and decorate with charms, beads, and raffia. Type journaling, trim and color edges with metallic rub-ons. Slide journaling into pocket and attach names to frames with circle clips. Create pull-out elements by placing patterned paper on black cardstock, cut with pull tab in the middle. Mount various pictures behind frames and adhere to patterned paper. Cut slits in a separate piece of black cardstock at the top and bottom. Add extensions on each panel as stoppers when pulled out. Place buttons embellished with raffia on each tab of panel. Adhere original page over panels, using foam tape along the top and bottom.

Denise Tucker, Versailles, Indiana

Supplies: Patterned papers (Anna Griffin, C-Thru Ruler, Scrap Ease); mesh (Magic Scraps); charms (Boutique Trims); buttons (Hillcreek Designs, Making Memories); beads (Beadery); premade frames (Ink Jet Art); metallic rub-ons (Craf-T); letter stamps (PSX Design); circle clips; black cardstock; raffia; vellum; stamping ink; embossing powder; eyelets; brads

Bewitched

In preparation for Halloween, Nancy's granddaughter enjoyed running around with a witch's hat on and a flashlight in hand. Trim and crumple patterned papers; flatten. Apply ink to navy and gray patterned paper and place on black cardstock. Adhere brown gingham patterned paper on left side of page. Mat photo on orange cardstock and layer on gingham. Accent with black fringe and sheer ribbon. Punch dragonfly shape from patterned paper rectangle and add name with typewriter letter stickers. Accent page with piece of net, buttons and ghost sticker. Layer netting and vintage Halloween image on corrugated cardstock, attach sheer ribbon to cardstock and layer on page over skeleton leaf. Create title with letter stickers and accent with fibers.

Nancy McCoy, Gulfport, Mississippi

Supplies: Patterned papers (Graphic Products Corp., Paper Patch); orange letter stickers (source unknown); typewriter letter stickers (EK Success); vintage Halloween image (source unknown); black and orange cardstocks; stamping ink; buttons; netting; ribbon; fringe; dragonfly punch

Halloween Is a Scary Thing

Sheila's computer-generated layout compares a current photo of her granddaughter with one taken when she was younger. In a paint program, apply a texturized gradient to the colors black, yellow and orange for page background. Scan measuring tape and open image in paint program. Add to right side and bottom of background. Use a custom brush to create tag; apply custom gradient and texture. Create fibers using the paintbrush tool and several preset fiber options. Type journaling on tag. When finished with design, copy and open with image-editing software. Open picture files, make black-and-white, clip subjects from their backgrounds and layer on page background. Type title.

Sheila McIntosh Dixon, Milton, Florida

Supplies: Image-editing software (Adobe Photoshop Elements, Microsoft Picture It Digital Image Pro); paint program (Jasc Paint Shop Pro)

Pumpkin Patch

Melanie hand-tinted her photo to add an original touch to her design. Mat enlarged photo with tan, orange and green cardstocks; adhere to tan page. For border, cut small tan rectangles and accent with chalk and black pen. Adhere rectangles to orange and green strips. Punch holes across strip and weave twine through. Print title on tan paper and tear edges. Use metal letters and a concho to create the first letter of each word in the title. Mat on orange cardstock and attach with circle clips.

Melanie Bruner, Knoxville, Tennessee

Supplies: Concho (Scrapworks); metal letter and circle clips (Making Memories); photo-tinting ink (Creative Photo Tinting); green, orange and tan cardstocks; twine; chalk

Pumpkins

A piece of artwork inspired Veronica's page. Crumple orange cardstock, flatten and attach to red cardstock with eyelets. Enlarge photo, crop corners and adhere to background at an angle. Color mesh ribbon with stamping ink and place along bottom of page. Attach photo to cardstock mat with eyelets and accent with jute. Add leaf stickers to orange cardstock and print journaling over them. Trim journaling, mat on red cardstock and accent with eyelets and jute.

Veronica Hugger, Houston, Texas

Supplies: Textured cardstocks (Artistic Scrapper, Bazzill); mesh ribbon (Pulsar); jute (Darice); leaf stickers (Me & My Big Ideas); eyelets; stamping ink

Fall at the Patch

Image-editing software allowed Jill to make the pumpkins in her photos stand out. Cut strips of black paper and layer on patterned paper background. Stamp words on twill tape and staple tape across both pages. Alter photos with image-editing software, print out, crop and adhere to page. Mat one photo with black paper. Adhere letter stickers to background and tag for title; accent tag with ribbon. Attach pumpkin embellishments to black strip. Journal with black pen.

Jill Beamer, Vancouver, British Columbia, Canada

Supplies: Patterned paper (Chatterbox); pumpkin embellishments (EK Success); word stickers (Creative Imaginations); ribbon (Impress Rubber Stamps); tag (Making Memories); letter stamps (Hero Arts, PSX Design); black cardstock; image-editing software; twill tape; foam tape; black pen

Guts

Not afraid to get his hands dirty, Sam's little boy dug right in to clean out the pumpkins. Stamp month randomly on tag and add word tag and twine. Adhere tag to patterned background. Attach brads down sides of page. Tear the edges of select pictures and ink the edges. Adhere pictures at angles, overlapping slightly. Knot twine and spread across page, taping ends to back of page. Add mini clothespins. Journal on tag and tie tag to twine.

Sam Cousins, Trumbull, Connecticut

Supplies: Patterned paper (Pixie Press); date stamp and brads (Making Memories); word tag (Chronicle Books); tinted tags and twine (Designer's Llibrary); black pen; clothespins; stamping inks

We gave Conner the task of naming our pumpkin. He named it Goliah (go-LIE-a) which, apparently is a clown on Jo-Jo's Circus. I thought it was hilarious when he told me that the pumpkin lived in a cave. What a funny kid.

October 2003

Our Pumpkin's Name is *Goliah* ... he lives in a cave

Although last year Conner had some serious issues with the whole pumpkin carving process, he seemed a little better this year. Although he wasn't a big fan of the pumpkin "guts" he didn't scream like a lady when Drew started cutting in with the knife. He still didn't really want to get too close to the pumpkin for a picture, especially when it was dark. Who knows what goes on in this little guy's head.

Goliah

Hilary's son named the family jack-o'-lantern Goliah, which she used as her page title. Print journaling on peach cardstock. Cut strips of orange cardstock and layer through center of background. Print title on cream cardstock and mount over strips. Mat one photo on black cardstock and both photos to page.

Hilary Erickson, Santa Clara, California

Supplies: Orange textured cardstocks (Bazzill)

Facts & Legends:

As the story goes, when a greedy Irish drunkard named Jack died, he was not allowed into heaven and not allowed into hell because of a trick he once played on the Devil. To light his way as he wandered the Earth, Jack made a lantern by placing a candle inside a hollowed-out turnip. (Irish immigrants, upon arrival in America, found that pumpkins made much better jack-o'-lanterns than the turnips they'd used in their homeland.)

Try This:

For a humorous page, have your family attempt to carve a turnip or two in addition to your annual Halloween pumpkin. Photograph the process and journal the pros and cons of carving turnips versus pumpkins.

Supplies: Patterned, leather and velvet papers (K & Company); eyelets (Happy Hammer); jewelry fittings (Westrim); die-cut letters (QuicKutz); paint (Delta); gold leaf pen (Krylon); blue cardstock; stamping ink; chalk; foam core; walnut ink

On Behalf of a Grateful Nation

In honor of Veteran's Day, Kelli's sons' boy scout troop took a trip to a veteran's cemetery. Tear patterned paper and ink the edges with stamping ink. Layer on cardstock. Mat photos on gray cardstock and ink the edges. Create photo corners using leather paper and brass eyelets. Adhere photos to one side of spread. Die cut letters from velvet paper for title; adhere letters under photos. To create frame for enlarged photo, cut strips of foam core and wrap with leather paper. Adhere metal jewelry accessories at corners of the frame. Print journaling on transparencies. Cut journaling apart and paint the back of transparencies with acrylic paint.

Kelli Noto, Centennial, Colorado

Duty Honor Country

Denise created a layout to pay tribute to those who fight for our freedom. First, cut premade flag photo border in half and coat with liquid glue. Crumple tissue paper and place over glue. Once dry, apply metallic rub-ons to tissue. Attach blue cardstock and enlarged photo on burgundy cardstock background. Print words on cream paper, trim into strips, add rub-ons to edges, attach star punches and adhere to page. Layer with flag borders. Create title by placing letter stickers on black craft foam and outlining with a craft knife. Apply metallic rub-ons and two coats of crystal lacquer. Place letters on tags cut from patterned paper and cardstock. Accent with painted star brads and adhere to page with foam tape.

Denise Tucker, Versailles, Indiana
Photo: Mary Margaret Moorhead, Versailles, Indiana

Supplies: Patterned paper (Karen Foster Design); premade flag border (Creative Imaginations); craft foam (Darice); letter stickers (Chatterbox); star punch (McGill); metallic rub-ons (Craf-T); crystal lacquer (Plaid); liquid glue (USArtQuest); blue and burgundy cardstocks; tissue paper; brads; acrylic paint

Thanksgiving

Thanksgiving Marriott Style

Sam's family usually has Thanksgiving dinner at her in-laws' house, but the year they moved to Florida, the family had a nontraditional holiday meal at a hotel. Adhere photos to patterned paper background. Tear a piece of patterned paper and ink the edges; layer over top photo. Roll polymer clay into small balls, flatten and press in letter stamps. Bake clay according to package directions and add color with stamping ink. Embellish envelope with premade letters, buttons and twine. Apply walnut ink to tag, let dry and journal on tag. Place inside envelope. Embellish design with buttons, fabric labels and brads.

Sam Cousins, Trumbull, Connecticut

Supplies: Patterned paper (Karen Foster Design); clay (Polyform Products); letter stamps (All Night Media); tag, envelope, premade letters and twine (Designer's Library); fabric labels (Me & My Big Ideas); brads; stamping ink; walnut ink; buttons; black pen

Thanksgiving

Bethany conveyed what she is most thankful for on strips of patterned and solid paper. Trim red paper, mount on oatmeal cardstock and layer photo over red. Cut four 1" strips of patterned and colored papers. Ink the edges with gold ink and attach below photo with brads. Add letter stickers and stamps for title and journaling. Accent with 3-D tag stickers.

Bethany Fields, Amarillo, Texas
Photo: Chris Cowan, Brookline, Massachusetts

Supplies: Patterned papers (EK Success, Karen Foster Design); letter stickers (Creative Imaginations); 3-D tag stickers (EK Success); letter stamps (Hero Arts); red and oatmeal cardstocks; stamping ink; brads

Thankful for My History

Pam used a heritage photo to represent her thankfulness for family. Fold beige cardstock to make creases, flatten and apply walnut ink for page background. Tear patterned papers, chalk the edges and layer on background. Mat photo with vintage photo frame and burgundy cardstocks; accent with photo corners. Ink the edges of photo mat with brown ink. Use pinking sheers to cut strips of fabric and hand stitch strips to background. Cover fabric with die-cut letters and journaling printed on a transparency. Stamp images on a tag and layer with patterned papers, metal word sticker, film, fibers and a photo corner. Using metal stamps, add date to metal tag and add to tag. Punch small circles and adhere each to appropriate person in photo.

Pam Sivage, Georgetown, Texas

Supplies: Patterned papers (Provo Craft); patterned vellum (NRN Designs); metal tag (FoofaLa); die cut letters (QuicKutz); metal letter stamps (Making Memories); flower stamp (Close To My Heart); fibers (Fibers by the Yard); metal word sticker (EK Success); beige and burgundy cardstocks; tag; photo corners; walnut ink

Give Thanks

Sheila repeated a photo of her granddaughter praying to illustrate the spirit of Thanksgiving. Draw background square with image-editing software. Fill square with a soft purple gradient. Apply cave painting filter to add texture to the background. Copy background shape, adjust size and center a smaller square over the background. Lighten background of smaller square. Open photo file and apply VM Extravaganza filter effect called Picture in a Picture. Copy photo nine times and adjust colors. Move photos inside smaller square. Type title and journaling. Create tags by creating circles in paint program; draw fibers using the paintbrush tool.

Sheila McIntosh Dixon, Milton, Florida

Supplies: Image-editing software (Photoshop Elements by Adobe, Picture It Digital Image Pro by Microsoft); paint program (Paint Shop Pro by Jasc)

Supplies: Orange, white and blue cardstocks

Thanksgiving Shared With Friends

Kristen adapted a design from a Starbucks sticker to create her Thanksgiving layout. Cut strips of light and dark orange cardstocks and layer over opposite shade background. Format title and journaling to print on green and black backgrounds; trim edges in wavy lines and crooked angles. Crop photos, mat on blue cardstock and adhere to page.

Kristin Holly, Glendale, Arizona

Tired Turkeys

Sherri recorded a common Thanksgiving occurrence in her family—after-dinner napping. Trim edges of beige cardstock, stamp images and layer on brown background. Accent each corner with a mini brad. Cut strips of corrugated cardstock and apply color with chalk-finish stamping ink. Cut ends of strips diagonally and use to frame one photo. Mat remaining photos on brown cardstock and place at angles on the page. Print journaling on cream cardstock, ink the edges, mat on brown cardstock and accent with brads. Print title on patterned paper and cut into tag shapes. Layer tags on brown cardstock and accent with eyelets, fibers and brads.

Sherri Brady, Victoria, British Columbia, Canada

Supplies: Brown textured cardstock (Bazzill); patterned paper (Karen Foster Design); stamp (Stampendous); tag (7 Gypsies); corrugated cardstock; stamping ink; brads; fibers; eyelets

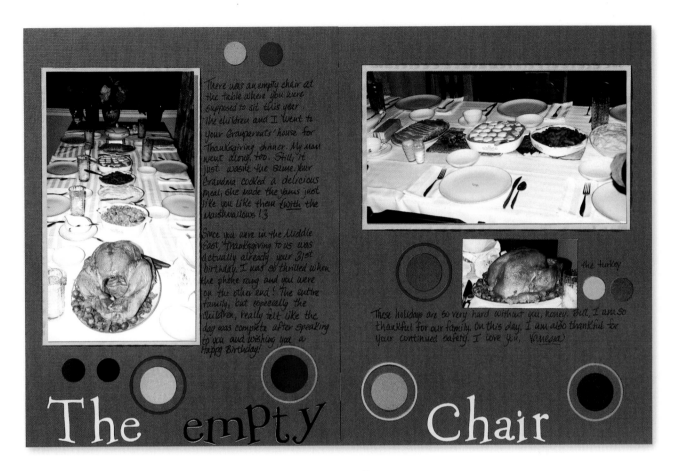

The handwritten journaling reads:

There was an empty chair at the table where you were supposed to sit this year. The children and I went to your Grandparents' house for Thanksgiving dinner. My mom went along, too. Still, it just wasn't the same. Your Grandma cooked a delicious meal; she made the yams just like you like them (with the marshmallows)!

Since you were in the Middle East, Thanksgiving to us was actually already your 31st birthday. I was so thrilled when the phone rang and you were on the other end! The entire family, but especially the children, really felt like the day was complete after speaking to you and wishing you a Happy Birthday!

These holidays are so very hard without you, honey. But, I am so thankful for our family. On this day, I am also thankful for your continued safety. I love you, Vanessa

the turkey

The empty Chair

Supplies: Brown textured cardstock (Bazzill); letter stickers and circle rub-ons (Creative Imaginations); black pen

Empty Chair

With her husband in the Middle East, Vanessa's family celebrated Thanksgiving with one empty place at the table. Mat photos on gold cardstock and place on brown background. Apply circle rub-ons throughout. Create title using letter stickers and journal on background with a black pen.

Vanessa Spady, Virginia Beach, Virginia

Facts & Legends:

Only 50 of the 100 original Pilgrims that came to America survived the first harsh winter in Plymouth, Massachusetts. A year later, the first Thanksgiving in the United States was celebrated in 1621. The Pilgrims, who came from England seeking religious freedom, invited Chief Massasoit and his braves to feast with them in hopes of strengthening their friendship with the Native Americans. The Native Americans sent ahead five deer for the feast, and the colonists provided wild turkeys, ground meal for corn bread and cooked cranberries. While early Americans continued to celebrate a feast of thanksgiving over the years on varying days, Thanksgiving Day became an official holiday during Lincoln's presidency in 1863.

Try This:

For journaling, include excerpts from President Lincoln's 1863 proclamation that established Thanksgiving Day. Find it by searching for "Lincoln + Thanksgiving" on an Internet search engine.

Gratitude

Maureen displayed her blessings by matting tiny pictures cut from her index print. For left page, cut a strip of green cardstock and adhere to patterned paper. Randomly place skeleton leaves throughout. Mat photo on brown and red cardstocks and accent with fibers; adhere to page. Tear brown cardstock and ink the edges with gold. Add letter stickers and leaf button. Print journaling on vellum and ink the edges. For right page, layer a strip of patterned paper on tan cardstock. Mat each index print and place on punched squares. Attach around edges of background with gold brads. Trim and tear mulberry paper and tan cardstock; adhere to center of page and layer with skeleton leaf. Print journaling on a transparency and attach over papers with nailheads. Accent with fibers and leaf button.

Maureen Spell, Carlsbad, New Mexico

Supplies: Patterned paper (Provo Craft); letter stickers (K & Company); fibers (Fibers by the Yard); mulberry paper (Paperbilities); nailheads (Westrim); leaf button (Jesse James); stickers (EK Success); green, brown and tan cardstocks; brads; square punch; stamping ink; transparency; vellum

Be Thankful

Ashlyn created a layout without photos to describe what she is thankful for. Using a craft knife, cut windows in maroon cardstock. Apply embossing ink and gold embossing powder to certain areas of cardstock and heat. Layer cardstock over patterned paper. Tear and chalk edges of various patterned papers and layer over maroon cardstock. Print journaling on cream cardstock, tear into squares and apply chalk; attach to page with eyelets. Die cut title letters, apply gold embossing powder and heat. Dye vellum tags with coffee and print words onto tags. Attach tags to page with eyelets.

Ashlyn Williamson, Sandersville, Georgia

Supplies: Patterned papers (7 Gypsies, K & Company, Rusty Pickle); die-cut letters (QuicKutz); vellum tags (Making Memories); chalk (Craf-T); maroon cardstock; embossing ink; embossing powder; eyelets

Supplies: Patterned vellum (C-Thru Ruler);
patterned paper (Club Scrap); mesh paper
(Magenta); fibers (Fibers by the Yard); twine,
wooden sticks and circles (www.scrapfindings.com);
metallic rub-ons (Craf-T); number stamps (PSX
Design); dimensional adhesive; brown, gold and
terra cotta cardstocks; stamping ink; black pen

5 Kernels Legend

Maegan's family incorporates an adapted version
of a Pilgrim legend into their own Thanksgiving
traditions. Tear patterned vellum and adhere
to terra cotta cardstock; layer with black mesh.
Mat photos on gold and brown cardstocks, tear
some edges and apply metallic rub-ons. Adhere
to background and detail edges with black pen.
Print journaling on patterned paper, cut into
blocks and strips; add rub-ons to edges. Stamp
numbers on small wooden circles and use to
accent journaling strips. To create title, cut a
3" wide strip of tan cardstock and attach seven
eyelets to each end. Thread fibers through eyelets and tape all ends to back of strip on both
sides. Insert small wooden sticks, weaving them
over and under the fibers. Cut out title letters
with a craft knife and adhere to thin strip of tan
cardstock; set eyelets on both ends. Attach strip
over wooden sticks with dimensional adhesive.
Layer title on mesh and adhere to background.

Maegan Hall, Virginia Beach, Virginia

Complete List of Holidays

Just like there is always a holiday or two that you wish you had more time to prepare for, there are a few lesser-known holidays that we didn't have room to represent in this book. Let this list serve as a reference while the holidays written on your wall calendars become covered with pencil-scratched reminders of sporting events, business meetings and doctor's appointments.

January

New Year's Day, January 1

Epiphany, January 6

National Mentoring Day, January 15

Martin Luther King, Jr. Day, date varies, third Monday

Chinese New Year, date varies

February

Groundhog Day, February 2

Lincoln's Birthday, February 12

Valentine's Day, February 14

President's Day, February 16

Washington's Birthday, February 22

Ash Wednesday, date varies, six Sundays fall between Ash Wednesday and Easter

March

Purim, date varies

St. Patrick's Day, March 17

Spring begins, March 20

Mothering Sunday (Canada), date varies

April

April Fools' Day, April 1

Palm Sunday, date varies, Sunday before Easter

Passover, date varies

Good Friday, date varies, Friday before Easter

Easter, date varies

Tax Day, April 15

Administrative Professionals Day, date varies, last Wednesday of a full week

Earth Day, April 22

May

Cinco de Mayo, May 5

National Day of Prayer, date varies, first Thursday

Nurses Day, May 6

Mother's Day, date varies, second Sunday

Armed Forces Day, date varies, third Saturday

Ascension, date varies

Victoria Day (Canada), date varies, Monday in late May

Memorial Day, date varies, last Monday

June

Flag Day, June 14

Summer begins, June 21

Father's Day, date varies, third Sunday

July

Canada Day, July 1

Independence Day, July 4

August

Friendship Day, date varies, first Sunday

Assumption, August 15

September

Labor Day, date varies, first Sunday

Patriot Day, September 11

Grandparents Day, date varies, Sunday after Labor Day

Rosh Hashanah, date varies

Citizenship Day, September 17

Autumn begins, September 22

Yom Kippur, date varies

October

National Children's Day, date varies, second Sunday

Clergy Appreciation Day, second Sunday

Thanksgiving (Canada), date varies, second Monday

Columbus Day, October 11

National Boss Day, October 16

Sweetest Day, date varies, third Saturday

United Nations Day, October 24

Halloween, October 31

November

All Saint's Day, November 1

Election Day, date varies, first Tuesday

Remembrance Day (Canada), November 11

Veterans Day, November 11

Thanksgiving, date varies, last Thursday

First Day of Advent, date varies

December

Hanukkah begins, date varies

Winter begins, December 21

Christmas, December 25

Kwanzaa begins, December 26

Boxing Day (Canada), December 26

Source: www.hallmark.com

Fact and Legend Resources

New Year's, p. 17

www.timessquare.com

Boxing Day, p. 19

www.factmonster.com,
www.kidsdomain.com

Valentine's Day, p. 21

www.greetingcard.org, www.udel.edu,
www.urbanlegends.about.com,
www.oldfashionedliving.com

St. Patrick's Day, p. 24

Adair, Daryl and Cronin, Mike. *The Wearing of The Green: A History of St. Patrick's Day.* London and New York: Routledge, 2002.

Hanukkah, p. 28

Cooper, Ilene. *Jewish Holidays All Year Round.* New York: Harry N. Abrams, Inc. Publishers, 2002.

Christmas, p. 43

www.Greetingcard.org,
www.thomasnast.com, www.santalady.com

Christmas, p. 48

Tompert, Ann. *St. Nicholas.* Honesdale, Pennsylvania: Boyds Mills Press, 2000.
www.catholic.org, www.santalady.com

Kwanzaa, p. 31

Santino, Jack. *All Around the Year: Holidays & Celebrations in American Life.* Urbana and Chicago: University of Illinois Press, 1994.

Passover, p. 53

Cooper, Ilene. *Jewish Holidays All Year Round.* New York: Harry N. Abrams, Inc. Publishers, 2002.

Easter, p. 61

Arthur, Mildred H. *Holidays of Legend.* New York: Harvey House, Inc., 1971.
www.geocities.com/Heartland/8149/egg.html\, www.informationentertainment.com/Holidays/easter.html

Mother's Day, p. 68

www.bbc.co.uk/religion, www.motheringsunday.com, www.21stcenturyplaza.com

Memorial Day, p. 71

www.rootsweb.com, Santino, Jack. *All Around the Year: Holidays & Celebrations in American Life.* Urbana and Chicago: University of Illinois Press, 1994.

Father's Day, p. 74

www.brownielocks.com,
www.web-holidays.com

Canada Day, p. 79

www.canoe.ca, www.canada.gc.ca

4th of July, p. 85

www.Usacitylink.com, Bensguide.gpo.gov, www.af.mil/stories, www.pueblo.gsa.gov/cic_text/misc/ourflag/greatseal.htm

Labor Day, p. 92

Santino, Jack. *All Around the Year: Holidays & Celebrations in American Life.* Urbana and Chicago: University of Illinois Press, 1994.

Grandparents Day, p. 95

www.hallmark.com,
www.grandparents_day.com

Halloween, p. 104

www.illusions.com/Halloween, www.urbanlegends.about.com, www.hallmark.com, www.washingtonpost.com, http://lcweb.loc.gov/folklife/html

Halloween, p. 114

http://www.vrmetro.com/halloween/lore.html, www.hallmark.com
Arthur, Mildred H. *Holidays of Legend.* New York: Harvey House, Inc., 1971.

Thanksgiving, p. 119

Arthur, Mildred H. *Holidays of Legend.* New York: Harvey House, Inc., 1971.
Santino, Jack. *All Around The Year: Holidays & Celebrations in American Life.* Urbana and Chicago: University of Illinois Press, 1994.

Additional Supplies and Instructions

Cover

Jodi Amidei, Memory Makers Books

Photos: Shannon Taylor, Bristol, Tennesee; Kelli Noto, Centennial, Colorado; Becky Harold, Lafayette, Colorado

Adhere sheer fabric over patterned paper. Cut thin frames from cardstock and stitch with beads and embroidery floss. Outline edges of frames with gold stamping ink. Cut letters from black using a template and stitch with beads. Cut tags from cardstock, add fibers, gold ink and adhere words printed on vellum. Accent tags with 3-D stickers, beads and handcut paper accents brushed with lacquer.

Supplies: Patterned paper (Provo Craft); 3-D stickers (EK Success); tag template (Quic-Kutz); crystal lacquer (Ranger); beads (Me & My Big Ideas); lettering template (Scrap Pagerz); stamping ink (Tsukineko); sheer material; green, black and red cardstocks

Bookplate, p. 3

Jodi Amidei, Memory Makers Books

Trim black cardstock and stitch around edges with beads. Cover slide mounts with patterned paper, add 3-D stickers; adhere to black cardstock with foam tape. Add glitter glue to select stickers and place others inside slide mounts. Tear piece of gold paper and adhere to black.

Supplies: Shiny black cardstock (Paper Adventures); patterned papers (Bo-Bunny Press, Provo Craft); 3-D stickers (EK Success); glitter glue (Ranger); beads (Westrim); gold vellum

Together at Christmas, p. 6

Photos: Michele Gerbrandt, Memory Makers

Trim edges of patterned papers and embossed vellum; layer on green background. Mat two photos on cream and attach to page. Print journaling on vellum and add to page. Adhere ribbon on left side and across bottom of page. Adhere vintage Christmas cut-outs to cardstock and distress with sandpaper; apply three seperate layers of extra thick embossing powder, heating each time. When dry, bend cardstock to form cracks in the enamel. Adhere images to page with foam tape. Die cut title letters from gold cardstock and adhere to ribbon with foam tape. Create gold frame from one

photo with decorative scissors and corner punch; adhere to page with foam tape. Add snowflake brads, fibers and string.

Supplies: Patterned papers (Provo Craft); embossed vellum (Paper Adventures); letter die cuts (QuicKutz); Christmas cut-outs (Design Originals); snowflake brads (Creative Impressions); corner punch (EK Success); die cut tag (Sizzix); ribbons (Jo-Ann Fabrics); extra thick embossing powder (Ranger); gold, cream and green papers; decorative scissors; fibers; stamping ink; transparency; foam tape

Adore, p. 12

Sam Cousins, Shelton, Connecticut

Tear patterned paper along each side and blot with black ink; mount on black cardstock. Mat photos on white cardstock and adhere to page. Accent with rub-on words applied in various directions. Embellish with red rickrack and heart sticker. To place emphasis on the word "kiss," tear word from patterned paper, ink edges, mat on black cardstock and cover with page pebble. Adhere with foam tape.

Supplies: Page pebble, rub-on words (Making Memories); dictionary patterned paper (7 Gypsies); heart sticker (EK Success); black cardstock; black ink; rickrack; foam tape

Believe In The Magic of Christmas, p. 12

Denise Tucker, Versailles, Indiana

Start by cutting a small rectangle inside a 12 x 12" piece of foam core with a craft knife. Layer red cardstock and cream embossed paper over foam core, cutting out rectangles over open space in foam core. Mount photos on embossed paper. Apply liquid adhesive over the word "magic" on printed transparency; press a gold leafing foil sheet over the word and pull sheet away. Layer transparency over top of page. Flip page over and fill rectangle with jingle bells. Attach small piece of embossed paper and sheet of cardstock over back of page to secure bells in shaker box. Print journaling on separate transparency, cut out, apply embossing powder over letters and heat emboss. Cut paper frames from red embossed paper, apply ink and gold powder

and heat emboss. Add paper frames around journaling and shaker box on top of printed transparency. Apply gold corner embellishments.

Supplies: Embossed papers (Provo Craft); transparency and foam core (Artistic Expressions); gold corner embellishments (Eggery Place); gold leaf foil sheets (Delta); extra thick embossing powder (Ranger); red cardstock; jingle bells

Happy New Year Baby, p. 12

Jennifer Bourgeault, Macomb Township, Michigan

Cut wide strip of patterned paper and adhere across bottom of green background. Print journaling on vellum and place over patterned paper. Cut a strip of brown cardstock and place along the top edge of vellum. Layer strips of light green and blue through center. Mat photos, round corners of one photo and adhere to page. Cut centers from two metal-rimmed tags, embellish two others with paper and mesh and add birthday hat stickers to each. To create the title, cut large circles from brown, green and blue cardstocks; layer. Using a craft knife cut the letters from white and green cardstocks. Add "happy" sticker banner for portions of the title.

Supplies: Patterned paper (SEI); tags (Making Memories); hat and banner stickers (EK Success); blue, brown, white, light and dark green cardstocks

Family Ties, p. 50

Trudy Sigurdson, Victoria, British Columbia, Canada
Photo: Phyllis Wright, Victoria, British Columbia, Canada

Cut 1½" strips of blue paper; miter the ends by cutting diagonally and ink all the edges. Piece strips together over pieces of thin foam; set aside. Mat photo on metal screen and cover the edges with paste. Using safety pins, attach screen to textured paper. Embellish with charms. Print journaling on vellum and attach with square brads. Adhere frame on top of textured paper and embellish with metal letters, label holder and ribbon.

Supplies: Patterned paper (Rusty Pickle); textured paper (Bazzill); metal letters, washer, brads, label holder and safety pin (Making Memories); ribbon (Offray); heart charm (Blue Moon Beads); jump ring; stamping ink; paste; vellum; metal screen

Dying Eggs, p. 50

Ruthann Grabowski, Yorktown, Virginia

Mat photos and adhere to patterned paper background. Attach fibers alongside two photos with brads. Write title, add egg punches, mat on purple and tear bottom edge.

Supplies: Patterned paper (Wübie); fibers (Ties That Bind); egg punch and writer and brush pens (EK Success); brads (Making Memories); purple, teal and green cardstocks

Mother's Day 2003, p. 50

Polly McMillan, Bullhead City, Arizona

Adhere ribbon along the bottom of blue cardstock. Tear patterned paper at an angle and adhere. Tear picture along one side and mount with photo corners. Embellish photo with ribbon and charms. Stamp journaling on patterned paper with letter stamps, tear along one side and attach with photo corners. For title, stamp on a tag and embellish with ribbon, label holder and charm. Embellish design with metal corner accents.

Supplies: Patterned paper (PSX Design); white ribbon and label holder (Magic Scraps); tag (Paperbilities); metal corner accents, heart charm and sunflower charm (www.maudeandmillie.com); letter stamps (Hero Arts, PSX Design); metal phrase (Making Memories); oval frame (Nunn Design); beige ribbon (Offray); metal word charm (source unknown); blue and cream cardstock

4th of July 2002, p. 76

Jeniece Higgins, Lake Forest, Illinois

Crumple two squares of patterned paper, flatten and adhere to blue cardstock. Cut and adhere mesh. Place red gingham ribbon across bottom of page. Machine stitch papers, mesh and ribbon to cardstock. Machine stitch flag to frayed denim and hand stitch denim over mesh. Mat photo on red cardstock and tear edges. Stitch square metal tiles with embroidery floss and adhere to mat. Use a metal engraver to draw flag on red metal and cover with metal frame. Stamp title onto premade wooden star. Accent page with star buttons, label tape and denim scraps.

Supplies: Flag patterned paper (K & Company); metal frame and metal tiles (Making Memories); letter stamps (PSX Design); buttons (Jesse James); label maker (Dymo); java weave (Jest Charming); blue and red cardstock; embroidery floss; paper wire; denim; wooden star; ribbon; fabric flag; mesh; flag toothpick; red metal sheet; stamping ink; engraving tool

The Thing About Grandparents, p. 76

Susan Cyrus, Broken Arrow, Oklahoma

Photos: Jane Bellinghausen, Hallsville, Missouri

Trim red patterned paper and layer at angles on tan cardstock. Machine stitch around outer edges. Print title on white cardstock and accent with a photo corner. Add other strips of white to background. Mat enlarged photo on vellum, adhere to page and add remaining photo. Print "grandparents" using computer fonts on white cardstock; cut out individual letters and place on the page. Print journaling on white cardstock, accent with photo corner and buttons; adhere to page. Crumple premade label and attach with cord; accent with buttons. Using a fine grit sand paper, lightly sand flower stickers and place throughout design.

Supplies: Patterned paper (Wordsworth); buttons (All My Memories); ribbon (Making Memories); stickers (Frances Meyer, Paper House Productions); premade label (Chatterbox); photo corners (Canson); tan and white cardstocks; embroidery floss; vellum; sand paper

Labor Day Picnic, p. 76

Lisa Dixon, East Brunswick, New Jersey

Cut strips of brown and red patterned paper and layer at the top and bottom of light green background. Mat photos on cream cardstock; ink the edges and layer on olive cardstock. Wrap pictures with scraps of fabric embellished with tags and safety pins; adhere to page. Print journaling on cream cardstock, ink the edges and layer on olive. Cut a strip of burlap and place along bottom. Cut title from inked cardstock using lettering templates. Scan plastic utensils, print on cardstock and place in folded red napkin. Wrap napkin with fabric and twine. Accent with 3-D food stickers.

Supplies: Patterned papers (Carolee's Creations, Pebbles, Rusty Pickle); 3-D food stickers (Westrim); eyelets (Impress Rubber Stamps); lettering template (C-Thru Ruler); cream, light and dark green cardstocks; black pen; stamping ink; safety pins; burlap; fabric; twine; paper napkin

With a Grateful Heart, p. 96

Pamela James, Ventura, California

Tear patterned paper and layer on pumpkin cardstock. Mat photo on cardstock and layer on green paper. Journal on tags and weave fibers throughout. Secure fibers with gold brads. Embellish tags with printed and stamped captions. Create title using die cut letters and shapes.

Supplies: Patterned paper (Karen Foster Design); fibers (EK Success); letter stamps (Hero Arts); die cut letters and heart (Sizzix); pumpkin, peach and tan cardstocks; brown pens; stamping ink

Sukkot, p. 96

Debbie DeMars, Overland Park, Kansas

Stamp words and images around the edges of tan cardstock in black ink. Layer black and white cardstocks over tan. Print journaling on vellum and adhere to one side of cork paper. Mat photos on white cardstock and adhere to cork paper. Accent journaling and cork with metal letters and corner accents.

Supplies: Cork paper (Magenta); metal letters and corner accents (Making Memories); stamps (Ma Vinci's, Stampin' Up!); tan, black and white cardstocks; stampin ink

Tricked, p. 96

Susan Cyrus, Broken Arrow, Oklahoma

Crop and mount photos on orange cardstock background. Type journaling, formatting the last word in a different color and font size. Print journaling on vellum. Outline "Tricked" with black pen and tear two edges of journaling. Apply black stamping ink to brads and adhere vellum to page with brads. Outline edges of background with black pen.

Supplies: Stamping ink (Tsukineko); brads (Making Memories); orange cardstock; black pen

Sources

The following companies manufacture products showcased on scrapbook pages within this book. Please check your local retailers to find these materials. We have made every attempt to properly credit the items mentioned in this book and apologize to those we may have missed.

7 Gypsies
(800) 588-6707
www.7gypsies.com

Accu-Cut® (wholesale only)
(800) 288-1670
www.accucut.com

Adobe
www.adobe.com

All My Memories
(888) 553-1998
www.allmymemories.com

All Night Media (see Plaid Enterprises)

All The Extras- no longer in business

American Art Clay Company (AMACO)
(800) 374-1600
www.amaco.com

American Crafts
(801) 226-0747
www.americancrafts.com

American Traditional Designs®
(800) 448-6656
www.americantraditional.com

Anna Griffin, Inc (wholesale only)
(888) 817-8170
www.annagriffin.com

Artistic Expressions
(219) 764-5158
www.artisticexpressionsinc.com

Artistic Scrapper
(818) 786-8304
www.artisticscrapper.com

Autumn Leaves (wholesale only)
(800) 588-6707
www.autumnleaves.com

Avery Dennison Corporation
(800) G0-AVERY
www.avery.com

Bazzill Basics Paper
(480) 558-8557
www.bazzillbasics.com

Beadery®, The
(401) 539-2432
www.thebeadery.com

Blue Moon Beads
(800) 377-6715
www.bluemoonbeads.com

Blumenthal Lansing
(201) 935-6220
www.buttonsplus.com

Bo-Bunny Press
(801) 771-0481
www.bobunny.com

Boutique Trims, Inc.
(248) 437-2017
www.boutiquetrims.com

Broderbund Software Corp.
(319) 247-3325
www.broderbund.com

Brother Sister Designs—no contact info available

Canson, Inc.®
(800) 628-9283
www.canson-us.com

CARL Mfg. USA, Inc. (wholesale only)
(800) 257-4771
www.Carl-Products.com

Carole Fabrics, Inc.
(706) 863-4742
www.carolefabrics.com

Carolee's Creations®
(435) 563-1100
www.carolees.com

Chatterbox, Inc.
(208) 939-9133
www.chatterboxinc.com

Chronicle Books
www.chroniclebooks.com

Close To My Heart®
(888) 655-6552
www.closetomyheart.com

Club Scrap™
(888) 634-9100
www.clubscrap.com

Cock-A-Doodle Design, Inc.
(800) 262-9727
www.cockadoodledesign.com

Colorbök™, Inc. (wholesale only)
(800) 366-4660
www.colorbok.com

Colors By Design
(800) 832-8436
www.colorsbydesign.com

Crafter's Workshop, The
(877) CRAFTER
www.thecraftersworkshop.com

Craf-T Products
(507) 235-3996
www.craf-tproducts.com

Create-a-Cut—no contact info available

Creative Imaginations (wholesale only)
(800) 942-6487
www.cigift.com

Creative Impressions
(719) 596-4860
www.creativeimpressions.com

Creative Memories®
(800) 468-9335
www.creativememories.com

Creative Photo Tinting
(619) 466-7236

Cropper Hopper™/Advantus Corporation (wholesale only)
(800) 826-8806
www.cropperhopper.com

C-Thru® Ruler Company, The (wholesale only)
(800) 243-8419
www.cthruruler.com

Daisy D's Paper Company
(888) 601-8955
www.daisydspaper.com

Darice, Inc.
(800) 321-1494
www.darice.com

Delta Technical Coatings, Inc.
(800) 423-4135
www.deltacrafts.com

Deluxe Designs
(480) 497-9005
www.deluxecuts.com

Designer's Library by Lana, The
(660) 582-6484
www.thedesignerslibrary.com

Design Originals
(800) 877-7820
www.d-originals.com

DieCuts with a View™
(801) 224-6766
www.diecutswithaview.com

DMD Industries, Inc. (wholesale only)
(800) 805-9890
www.dmdind.com

Doodlebug Design Inc.™
(801) 966-9952

Duncan Enterprises
(800) 782-6748
www.duncan-enterprises.com

Dymo
www.dymo.com

Eggery Place, The
www.theeggeryplace.com

EK Success™, Ltd. (wholesale only)
(800) 524-1349
www.eksuccess.com

Ellison® Craft & Design
(800) 253-2238
www.ellison.com

Emagination Crafts, Inc. (wholesale only)
(630) 833-9521
www.emaginationcrafts.com

Ever After Scrapbook Co.
(800) 646-0010

Fiber Scraps
(215) 230-4905
www.fiberscraps.com

Fibers by the Yard™
(405) 364-8066
www.fibersbytheyard.com

Fiskars, Inc. (wholesale only)
(715) 842-2091
www.fiskars.com

Foofala
(402) 330-3208
www.foofala.com

Frances Meyer, Inc.®
(800) 372-6237
www.francesmeyer.com

Friendly Fibers—no contact info available

Gifted Line, The
(800) 533-7263

Gotta Mesh™/ Notions Marketing
(616) 243-8424
www.gottamesh.com

Grafix® Graphic Art Systems, Inc. (wholesale only)
(800) 447-2349
www.grafixarts.com

Graphic Products Corporation
(800) 323-1660
www.gpcpapers.com

Griff's Shortcuts
(989) 894-5916
www.griffs-shortcuts.com

Hambly Studios, Inc.
(800) 451-3999
www.hamblystudios.com

Happy Hammer, The
(303) 690-3883
www.thehappyhammer.com

Hero Arts® Rubber Stamps, Inc. (wholesale only)
(800) 822-4376
www.heroarts.com

Hillcreek Designs
(619) 562-5799
www.hillcreekdesigns.com

Hirschberg, Schutz & Co., Inc.
(800) 221-8640

Hot Off The Press, Inc.
(800) 227-9595
www.paperpizazz.com

Imaginations—no contact info available

Impress Rubber Stamps
(206) 901-9101
www.impressrubberstamps.com

Ink Jet Art—no contact info available

Ivy Cottage Creations
(888) 303-1375
www.ivycottagecreations.com

Jasc Software
(800) 622-2793
www.jasc.com

Jesse James & Co., Inc.
(610) 435-0201
www.jessejamesbutton.com

Jest Charming
(702) 564-5101
www.jestcharming.com

Jo-Ann Fabrics & Crafts
(888) 739-4120
www.joann.com

Junkitz
(212) 944-4250
www.junkitz.com

K & Company
(888) 244-2083
www.kandcompany.com

Karen Foster Design™ (wholesale only)
(801) 451-9779
www.karenfosterdesign.com

KI Memories
www.kimemories.com

Kopp Design
(208) 656-0734
www.koppdesign.com

Kreinik Mfg. Co., Inc.
(800) 537-2166
www.kreinik.com

Krylon
(216) 566-2000
www.krylon.com

Lasting Impressions for Paper, Inc.
(801) 298-1979
www.lastingimpressions.com

Li'l Davis Designs
(949) 838-0344
www.lildavisdesigns.com

Liquitex® Artist Materials
(888) 4-ACRYLIC
www.liquitex.com

Loersch Corporation USA
(610) 264-5641
www.loersch.com

Lyons Co.—no contact info available

Magenta Rubber Stamps (wholesale only)
(800) 565-5254
www.magentarubberstamps.com

Magic Mesh™
(651) 345-6374
www.magicmesh.com

Magic Scraps™
(972) 238-1838
www.magicscraps.com

Making Memories
(800) 286-5263
www.makingmemories.com

Marvy® Uchida (wholesale only)
(800) 541-5877
www.uchida.com

Ma Vinci's Reliquary
www.crafts.dm.net

McGill, Inc.
(800) 982-9884
www.mcgillinc.com

Me & My Big Ideas (wholesale only)
(949) 589-4607
www.meandmybigideas.com

Memories Complete™, LLC
(866) 966-6365
www.memoriescomplete.com

Microsoft Corporation
www.microsoft.com

Missing Link Stamp Company, The
(425) 401-9903
www.missinglinkstamp.com

Mosaic Mercantile
(877) 9-MOSAIC
www.mosaicmercantile.com

Mrs. Grossman's Paper Co.
(wholesale only)
(800) 429-4549
www.mrsgrossmans.com

Mustard Moon™
(408) 229-8542
www.mustardmoon.com

My Daughter's Wish
www.mydaughterswish.com

My Mind's Eye™, Inc.
(801) 298-3709
www.frame-ups.com

NRN Designs
(800) 421-6958
www.nrndesigns.com

Nunn Design
(360) 379-3557
www.nunndesign.com

Office Max
www.officemax.com

Offray
www.offray.com

On The Surface
(847) 675-2520

Paper Adventures® (wholesale only)
(800) 727-0699
www.paperadventures.com

Paper Diva—no contact info available

Paper Fever, Inc.
(801) 412-0495
www.paperfever.com

Paper House Productions
(800) 255-7316
www.paperhouseproductions.com

Paper Illuzionz
(406) 756-9678
www.paperilluzionz.com

Paper Inspirations™
(406) 756-9678

Paper Parachute—no contact info
available

Paperbilities—no contact info available

Paper Patch®, The
(800) 397-2737
www.paperpatch.com

Patchwork Paper Design
(480) 515-0537
www.patchworkpaper.com

Pebbles, Inc.
(800) 438-8153
www.pebblesinc.com

Penny Black Inc.
(510) 849-1883
www.pennyblackinc.com

Pioneer Photo Albums, Inc.®
(800) 366-3686
www.pioneerphotoalbums.com

Pixie Press
(888) 834-2883
www.pixiepress.com

Plaid Enterprises, Inc.
(800) 842-4197
www.plaidonline.com

Polyform Products Co.
(847) 427-0020
www.sculpey.com

Pressed Petals
(800) 748-4656
www.pressedpetals.com

PrintWorks
(800) 854-6558
www.printworkscollection.com

Provo Craft® (wholesale only)
(888) 577-3545
www.provocraft.com

PSX Design™
(800) 782-6748
www.psxdesign.com

Pulsar Paper Products
(877) 861-0031
www.pulsarpaper.com

Punch Bunch, The
(254) 791-4209
www.thepunchbunch.com

QuicKutz®
(888) 702-1146
www.quickutz.com

Ranger Industries, Inc.
(800) 244-2211
www.rangerink.com

Renkly/PoliUSA, Inc.
(877) 4-RENKLY
www.renkly.com

Rubber Baby Buggy Bumpers
(970) 224-3499
www.rubberbaby.com

Rustic Treasures—no contact info
available

Rusty Pickle
(801) 272-2280   www.rustypickle.com

Sandylion Sticker Designs
(800) 387-4215
www.sandylion.com

Sarah Heidt Photo Craft
(734) 424-2776
www.SarahHeidtPhotoCraft.com

Sarah Lugg
www.sarahlugg.com

ScrapArts
(503) 631-4893
www.scraparts.com

Scrapbook Wizard™, The
(435) 752-7555
www.scrapbookwizard.com

Scrap Ease®
(800) 272-3874
www.whatsnewltd.com

Scrap Pagerz™
(435) 645-0696
www.scrappagerz.com

ScrapTherapy Designs, Inc.
(800) 333-7880
www.scraptherapy.com

Scrapworks, LLC
www.scrapworksllc.com

SEI, Inc.
(800) 333-3279
www.shopsei.com

Sizzix
(866) 742-4447
www.sizzix.com

Sonburn, Inc. (wholesale only)
(800) 527-7505
www.theroyalstore.com

Stamp Doctor, The
www.stampdoctor.com

Stampendous!®
(800) 869-0474
www.stampendous.com

Stampin' Up!®
(800) 782-6787
www.stampinup.com

Sticker Studio™
(208) 322-2465
www.stickerstudio.com

Suburban Paper—no contact info
available

Sweetwater
(800) 359-3094
www.sweetwaterscrapbook.com

Target
www.target.com

Ties That Bind—no contact info available

Timeless Touches/Dove Valley Prod. LLC
(623) 362-8285
www.timelesstouches.net

Tsukineko®, Inc.
(800) 769-6633
www.tsukineko.com

Two Busy Moms—see Deluxe Designs

USArtQuest
(800) 200-7848
www.usartquest.com

Watch Us, Inc.—no contact info available

Westrim® Crafts
(800) 727-2727
www.westrimcrafts.com

Wordsworth
(719) 282-3495
www.wordsworthstamps.com

Wright Designs—no contact info
available

Wubie Prints
(888) 256-0107
www.wubieprints.com

Index